T0131770

Cambridge Elements ≡

Elements in the Archaeology of Europe
edited by
Manuel Fernández-Götz
University of Edinburgh
Bettina Arnold
University of Wisconsin–Milwaukee

MEGASITES IN PREHISTORIC EUROPE

Where Strangers and Kinsfolk Met

Bisserka Gaydarska
Durham University

John Chapman
Durham University

European Association
of Archaeologists

CAMBRIDGE
UNIVERSITY PRESS

Shaftesbury Road, Cambridge CB2 8EA, United Kingdom

One Liberty Plaza, 20th Floor, New York, NY 10006, USA

477 Williamstown Road, Port Melbourne, VIC 3207, Australia

314–321, 3rd Floor, Plot 3, Splendor Forum, Jasola District Centre,
New Delhi – 110025, India

103 Penang Road, #05–06/07, Visioncrest Commercial, Singapore 238467

Cambridge University Press is part of Cambridge University Press & Assessment,
a department of the University of Cambridge.

We share the University's mission to contribute to society through the pursuit of
education, learning and research at the highest international levels of excellence.

www.cambridge.org
Information on this title: www.cambridge.org/9781009096607

DOI: 10.1017/9781009099837

First published 2022

A catalogue record for this publication is available from the British Library.

ISBN 978-1-009-09660-7 Paperback
ISSN 2632-7058 (online)
ISSN 2632-704X (print)

Additional resources for this publication at www.cambridge.org/megasites

Megasites in Prehistoric Europe

Where Strangers and Kinsfolk Met

Elements in the Archaeology of Europe

DOI: 10.1017/9781009099837
First published online: October 2022

Bisserka Gaydarska
Durham University

John Chapman
Durham University

Author for correspondence: Bisserka Gaydarska, b_gaydarska@yahoo.co.uk

Abstract: This is an Element about some of the largest sites known in prehistoric Europe – sites so vast that they often remain undiscussed for lack of the theoretical or methodological tools required for their understanding. Here, the authors use a relational, comparative approach to identify not only what made megasites but also what made megasites so special and so large. They have selected a sample of megasites in each major period of prehistory – Neolithic, Copper, Bronze and Iron Ages – with a detailed examination of a single representative megasite for each period. The relational approach makes explicit comparisons between smaller, more 'normal' sites and the megasites using six criteria: scale, temporality, deposition/ monumentality, formal open spaces, performance and congregational catchment. The authors argue that many of the largest European prehistoric megasites were congregational places.

Keywords: megasites, congregation, relational approach, Nebelivka, Alsónyék, Valencina de la Concepción, Corneşti, Bil'sk

ISBNs: 9781009096607 (PB), 9781009099837 (OC)
ISSNs: 2632-7058 (online), 2632-704X (print)

Contents

Preface   1

1 Introduction   2

2 Trypillia Megasites, Ukraine   13

3 Neolithic and Copper Age Sites in the Balkans
and Central Europe   24

4 Neolithic and Copper Age Sites in Southern Europe   42

5 Bronze Age Megasites   62

6 Iron Age Megasites - from Bil'sk to Bagendon   75

7 Discussion and Conclusions   98

References   107

A further Online Appendix (referred to in the text as OA/)
can be accessed at www.cambridge.org/megasites

Preface

Some people we know coped with COVID–19 enforced lockdowns by learning Mandarin Chinese, others by joining new Zoom meetings teaching the art of snake-charming, still others by beefing up their biceps and triceps and yet others by extending their capacity for consuming Cobra at all hours. We took the exciting alternative of writing a new book. Whether the mental well-being of people turning to the other strategies turns out to be better than ours, only time will tell. But we have coped reasonably well with the writing, even if data acquisition was at times harder than for any other book we have written, meaning that we leaned heavily on friends and colleagues for references not readily found in the generally excellent Bill Bryson Library at Durham University.

When Manuel Fernández-Götz and Bettina Arnold approached us to write about megasites in European prehistory, they had a fair idea of where we would be coming from – the Trypillia megasites of Ukraine. Part of that research was already published by Bisserka in books that Manuel had edited. But extending our compass from the Ukrainian Neolithic to the whole of European prehistory proved a challenging task. Responding to that challenge within the scope of the 'Elements' format meant the selection of a small but perfectly formed group of megasites from different eras. So how did we choose the megasites?

The starting point of the Element was clearly the megasites that we had studied in great detail before – the Trypillia megasites of the Ukraine. The choice of the next example – Alsónyék, in western Hungary – came about as a direct result of Bisserka's engagement with the site in the 'Times Of Their Lives' Project (or ToTL), for which she worked as a part-time post-doctoral research assistant. The ToTL connection was also important for the choice of Valencina de la Concepción. While Bisserka did not work on the Valencina chronology, we had both met the director, Professor Leonardo García Sanjuán, at the Second Shanghai Archaeological Forum and enjoyed many discussions with him on Eurasian urbanism. Later, Bisserka edited an article that he published on Valencina in her special issue on urbanism in the *Journal of World Prehistory*. Both of us had enjoyed several discussions with our friend Anthony Harding on the Bronze Age Cornești megasite, whose special characteristics and immense size made it an obvious choice. The final megasite – the Iron Age complex at Bil'sk – was a site that we had encountered – though never visited – during our Ukrainian Project and it was obvious that we could not exclude the largest hillfort known in prehistoric Europe. As with the Trypillia megasites in the 2000s, the predominant languages of Russian and Ukrainian in which Bil'sk was published meant that it was poorly understood in the West. This left some obvious candidates that we should enjoy researching.

And that is what we have done. The task of extending our chronological and cultural range by looking at sites we should not normally have analysed in such detail was a pleasurable experience. We hope that readers will detect something of that enjoyment in our account and themselves share in some of the excitement of grappling with such a class of sites.

1 Introduction

1.1 From Silicon Valley to Stanwick

Governments, universities and land developers take the term 'megasite' to mean an enhanced zone with strong infrastructure, shovel-ready for the creation of a new business cluster. The first such megasite, at Stanford University, grew into Silicon Valley. Meanwhile, in prehistoric Europe – a continent with a late development of urban centres in the 1st millennium BC – larger-than-usual sites emerged and disappeared without causing much long-term cultural impact but also without prompting explanation. It is only in the last two decades that megasites have been recognised as an interesting phenomenon worth attention (e.g., in Iberia: Martínez-Sevilla et al. 2020). But even when megasites have stimulated research projects, remarkably little attention has been paid to why the sites were so large (e.g., Cornești: Heeb et al. 2017). Moreover, and with the exception of Roland Fletcher's research (1995; see Section 1.1), the tendency in megasite studies for investigations in terms of their own local cultural context has precluded comparative approaches.

In this Element, we use a relational, comparative approach to identify not only what made megasites but also what made megasites so special and so large. We address three themes in this Element – megasites in general, the phenomenon of congregation and five examples of special megasites. Congregation consisted of formal meetings at various scales according to punctuated temporality – people congregated at the congregation place and then left. This occurred not only at megasites but also at smaller sites, such as *Rondels* (see Section 3) but the scale of congregation events at megasites attracted particularly large numbers of the strangers and kinsfolk – those prehistoric forbears of C. P. Snow's Cambridge fellows and citizens in his *Strangers and Brothers* series, dealing with life and times in the colleges and the town and examining issues of personal power and integrity. The size of the Element limits our study to a consideration of one class of megasites (the Trypillia megasites) plus one megasite per period (Neolithic, Copper, Bronze and Iron Ages), with each megasite contextualised through a brief socio-cultural introduction (Fig. 1). By the end of this Element, we hope that readers will have come to understand why megasites in European prehistory mattered and how they can help us to reach a deeper understanding of prehistoric societies in Europe.

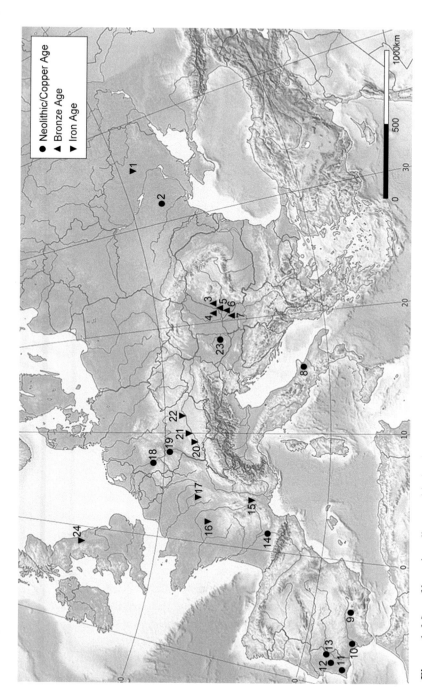

Figure 1 Map of key sites discussed in book: 1 – Bil'sk; 2 – Nebelivka; 3 – Cornești; 4 – Csanádpalota; 5 – Munar; 6 – Sântana; 7 – Idjoš – Gradište; 8 – Foggia Plain sites (Passo di Corvo, Motta di Lupo, Masseria Fragella & Posta d'Innanzi; 9 – Marroquíes – Bajos; 10 – Valencina de la Concepción; 11 – Alcalar; 12 – Porto Torrão; 13 – Perdigões; 14 – Villeneuve – Tolosane & St. Michel-du-Touche; 15 – Corent; 16 – Bourges; 17 – Mont Lassois; 18 – Urmitz; 19 – Wiesbaden – Schierstein; 20 – Heuneburg; 21 – Heidengraben; 22 – Kelheim; 23 – Alsónyék; 24 – Stanwick (source: authors, re-drawn by Lauren Woodard)

Anyone reflecting on a research strategy for a 450 ha site will immediately realise that these sites are challenging to investigate – that we shall always rely on exploration of only a tiny fraction of their surface area. In this sense, writing this account would have been impossible without the huge advances in geophysical investigations in the last two decades, which have provided crucial detail for megasite internal layouts. But, however indispensable, geophysical plots do not provide chronological detail and it is only with targeted excavation and Accelerator Mass Spectometry (AMS) dating through projects such as 'The Times of Their Lives' (or 'ToTL': Whittle 2018) that we can develop improved interpretation. These methodological issues remain as yet unresolved for several of the megasites we consider here. However, the point made in the study of Trypillia megasites – that the methodological advances would be compromised without parallel advances in theoretical understanding (Gaydarska 2020) – applies just as strongly to other megasites. But what do we mean by a prehistoric megasite?

1.2 Refining the theoretical framework for megasites

Our central proposition for investigation is that megasites constituted particularly large, though diverse, kinds of congregation places. Before we lay out the relational approach to megasites, it is important to define an appropriate terminology, for many terms are used, sometimes interchangeably, sometimes without definition. The five related terms regularly used in discussions of large settlements – 'nucleation', 'aggregation', 'agglomeration', 'assembly' and 'seasonal gathering' – do not adequately cover the sense of congregations. 'Nucleation' is contrasted with 'dispersion', often without a temporal dimension, while 'agglomeration' refers to the consolidation of a large, usually permanent population size. But not all agglomeration sites were necessarily congregation places if they lacked the motivation or the facilities for major meetings. The more neutral term 'aggregation' is used as much for a collection of structures, physical or social, as for large groups of people. The term 'assembly' prioritises the meeting aspect of a site without necessarily invoking an appropriately large scale. The term closest in spirit to congregation is 'seasonal gathering', in the sense of Wengrow and Graeber's (OA/2015; cf. OA/Wengrow 2019) demonstration that seasonal hunter-gatherer group size alternated between bands and large networks (viz., fusion–fission strategies), although, even with this term, the scale of meeting is rarely specified. The notion that sizeable 'seasonal gatherings' were normal for human populations in the Holocene, as at Göbekli tepe (OA /Schmidt 2006) or Lepenski Vir (OA/Srejović 1972), provides the key long-term context for congregation places.

In other words, not all megasites were congregation places, if they lacked meeting spaces, and vice versa, if they were too small. Moreover, while small sites often shared similar practices with large sites, the key difference was the intensity of the practices at the larger sites. Megasites can be considered as congregational places if they embodied combinations of great size and scale as well as intensity of practices in a relational sense. It is important to emphasise that absolute size can be misleading. For example, the ditches at the Southern French Chassey sites of Villeneuve-Tolosane enclosed 'only 25 ha' but this size exceeded the size of small 0.07 ha Chassey settlements by a factor of 400 (OA/ Phillips 1982)! The successive phases of the Iron Age site of Stanwick, North Yorkshire (UK) encapsulated the change from a congregation place to a megasite with regional congregations, with the earlier phases lacking the intensity of depositional practices so clearly attested in the final phase (OA/ Haselgrove 2016).

We can extend to much of the farming period in Europe the insight of Danielisová & Fernández-Götz (2015) that the later prehistoric and early historic world was still principally the world of the common farmer. Haselgrove et al. (2018) concur, proposing that the vast majority of settlements were small farmsteads with populations of fewer than 100 people. For Adler et al. (OA/1996: 403), local communities were aggregations of people, shared risks, inter-dependencies and identities, constituting the highest level of decision-making above the residential kinship level in non-stratified societies. The political implications of this insight is that the basic settlement units for most of prehistoric Europe were relatively autonomous segmentary societies, where the identities of equivalent settlement segments depended on opposition to such segments but whose social reproduction required their existence (OA/Curras & Sastre 2020), and which came together seasonally for larger-scale interaction. There was an evident political tension between decisions more related to the community level and those taken at the congregational scale. Any shift towards specialised site-based practices, such as regional congregations, at megasites would at once have weakened the independence of segmentary communities while strengthening the regional significance of megasites.

One such practice in which differences between segmentary communities and central places was played out was public architecture. A feature of each megasite was the scale and significance of its public architecture, which would have exceeded the scope of any village or farmstead constructions. However, as L. K. Harrison & Bilgen (OA/2019) remind us, architecture could be mobilised as an instrument of hierarchy or become an integrative medium of community building, insofar as the built environment represented the 'imagined ideologies' of the residents and visitors. We should recall that people began to self-identify as an integrated entity before – not after – major constructions, betokening a prior change in community ideology (OA/Ryan 2019: 341–2). Munro's (1997) inversion of the division of labour to become the labour of division is pertinent to the manipulation of architectural difference: architecture created spatial divisions in the light of the principle that 'the more divisive a society, the more space is divided' (OA/Fernández-Götz & Krausse 2016: 15). However, the converse is true of the large open space in many congregation places, where the absence of divisions created a welcoming reception to all participants.

There was also significant variability between megasites and smaller communities in the way that such constructions constituted 'the choreography of power' (OA/Osanna 2016: 275) – an idea related to Sharples's (OA/2007: 179–80) notion of 'labour as potlatch'. It will also be important to investigate the extent to which megasite ideological order was driven by a rhetoric of stability and permanence (OA/Riva 2020), as found in site planning, continuities in traditional architectural use of space or the monumental scale of ditches and ramparts, or whether, by contrast, there were important tensions between the maintenance of this rhetoric and its disruption through socio-economic changes.

Another long-term tension found in most, if not all, of the megasites featured here concerns the relations between the domestic and mortuary domains (OA/Chapman 1991) and, in particular, bodily mobility. In the context of well-established settlements, there is an assumption that most or all of the local deceased were buried nearby in specially constituted, permanent cemeteries. However, mobile forager sites and dispersed farming homesteads had a tethered relationship to their central cemeteries, with bodies regularly moved from the (sometimes seasonal) settlement to their permanent, ancestral place (e.g., megalithic tombs in much of western Europe). There is therefore a widespread precedent in time and place for the transport of the complete bodies of the deceased for burial across distances of 5–10 km to cemeteries and megalithic tombs. Another term for these places is a mortuary congregation. We should therefore expect to identify congregational site in the mortuary as well as in the domestic domain.

It is precisely the mortuary domain to which Munro's notion of the labour of division is pertinent in both the spatial and ontological senses. The centrality of the categorisation of the human body in these practices implies that the more varied the mortuary practices, the more different the ontologies of the persons buried. One way in which mortuary variability was played out was through the tension between the dominant mortuary practice and variations on, or oppositions to, the main practice. If we can recognise in the megasites a trend through time towards greater variability of mortuary practice, did this correlate not only with social differentiation but also with individualisation – with mortuary personalisation?

In summary, megasites as congregational places can be considered as special combinations of relational size, scale and intensity of practices. The sites that we shall examine here are examples of Fletcher's intermediate group of low-density settlements of between 1 and 100 km^2 (Fletcher 2019: 17). There is a long-term

Holocene contrast between smaller residential sites and larger (sometimes much larger) seasonal congregational sites. A major issue for consideration is the extent to which the community's loss of political autonomy (autarky) was offset through the scalar advantages pertaining to not just large but massive congregational centres. In the next section, we consider the relational approach to megasites as congregational centres.

1.3 The Relational Approach to Megasites

It will have become clear by now that the relational approach to megasites forms the foundation of the Element. One of the authors (B. Gaydarska) has developed this approach in her study of the low-density urbanism characteristic of the Trypillia megasites (OA/Gaydarska 2016; Gaydarska 2020, chapter 6) in an attempt to circumvent the inflexibilities of those urban studies dominated by high-density cities. Here, although the urban theme is not pursued further, the touchstone of the relational approach is what people experienced in 'normal', small settlements and what they experienced in megasites. It is a fundamental categorical mistake to assume that megasites were settlement sites writ very large; this is tantamount to assuming that aircraft carriers were simply very large versions of yachts.

One of the most complex issues for urban sites and megasites alike remains the currencies used for comparison. Standard units of analysis, such as Childe's criterion of writing (OA/Childe 1950), can readily become ossified and essentialised, while others, such as ideology or social power (OA/Cowgill 2004: 543), are too general for differentiating urban from non-urban. The parameters chosen in this study are as follows: scale, temporality, deposition/monumentality, formal open spaces, performance and congregational catchment. We claim that these six parameters provide a common frame of reference and an appropriate terminology for all of the megasites discussed here in detail. While accepting that there are other parameters that could have been considered, we suggest that there are good research reasons for the inclusion of these parameters.

1.3.1 Scale

Scale is a basic parameter of megasites – perhaps the most basic. For megasites that are also congregation places, a more useful analogy would be between parish churches and cathedrals: while congregations who met at both types of building could enjoy similar spiritual experiences, the parish church congregation was limited in the experiential scale of participation in the full range of practices typical of cathedrals. It will become clear in this Element that up-scaling was transformative *at all levels*. Elsewhere, we have discussed the implications of increased metrics in terms of resources, logistics and settlement planning (OA/Gaydarska

2019). Here, we focus on the various impacts of up-scaling, as they affected smaller and larger megasites. These effects can be divided into the positive, the negative and the neutral effects of up-scaling (Gaydarska & Chapman 2021).

The principal positive effect of up-scaling was the increase in the number, size and variation in interactions between kinsfolk, friends and strangers, often experienced through a greater population heterogeneity. These interactions offered the possibility of the development of cross-cutting identities not likely on small sites, leading to a wider range of enchained social relationships. One form of interaction was the observation and transmission of a wider pool of skills – especially specialised skills and knowledge – with the potential for the development of what J. E. Clark and Parry (OA/1990) termed 'conspicuous production' (e.g., fine painted wares, rock crystal weapons or ivory ornaments). The scale of feasting and ritual – far beyond that seen on smaller sites – brought novel experiences for the megasite visitors. However, the size of the megasites would not have made close interaction easy.

The negative effects of up-scaling can be subsumed under Greg Johnson's (1982) term 'scalar stress'. Higher site numbers would have produced more waste (both personal and household), more pollution (especially in local river and stream catchments), more noise and more illness (tuberculosis has been identified at Alsónyék, although claims that the plague was discovered at Trypillia megasites are incorrect). The diversity of viewpoints among the varied site residents and visitors would have constrained decision-making, emphasising the importance of the megasite 'Guardians' and making intra-site divisions into more manageable group-ings a priority. One area likely to have led to tension was the potential clash between the 'collective' identity of the megasite and the 'local' identities of the many visitors. The escalation of disagreements into conflict or even violence would have been a much more serious issue at megasites than at smaller settlements.

The neutral effects of up-scaling concerned those requirements that increased in line with growing populations: more food and water, building materials and fuel. These effects had a more profound effect in terms of organisation, logistics and human experience, with co-operative learning and action essential in tasks such as site maintenance, woodland management and hunting and gathering. Perhaps the key challenge for megasites was how to 'manage' issues of scale by bringing the positive experiences of a vast settlement down to a manageable 'local' scale.

In summary, up-scaling was transformative on a personal, community and network level. This transformative power was perhaps not immediately grasped at the very first massive gathering but with time was most certainly embraced and appreciated. This is what led to the formalisation of this experience in the establishment of megasites (OA/Gaydarska 2016).

1.3.2 Temporality

Temporality does not only refer to the overall duration of a megasite occupation, although this is always an important factor in a site's biography. Another important aspect of temporality concerns the debate over the assumption of long-term, uninterrupted, all-year-round permanence of megasites – an assumption that has now been challenged for many of the 'Anomalous Giant' sites (also termed 'Giants': Fletcher 2019) – sites that we would term 'megasites'.

The size and variability of megasites raise the possibility of the emergence of different temporalities on different parts of the megasite. We maintain that the dominant temporality on megasites was 'punctuated temporality', during which peaks of sociality (also termed 'timemarks': OA/Chapman 1997) stood out from everyday experiences and practices. Such timemarks were related to both natural and cultural rhythms (the solstices or the 'Beating of the Bounds' – the annual Mediaeval practice of marking the boundaries of the parish by processing round the perimeter (OA/Hindle 2016) – and were subject to varying durations (a small pit-digging or a special, day-long feast), *tempi* (varying intensity marked by more or less frequent events) and changes in rhythms (especially at the start and finish of major events). A 'staggered temporality' could have been introduced as a form of scheduling to ensure an even spread of resource requirements between households or neighbourhoods at times of peak resource demand. There are potential research benefits from the identification of varying temporalities between and within different megasites.

1.3.3 Deposition and Monumentality

Deposition and monumentality are both central aspects of our vision of megasites – the way that megasites were 'consumed' by kinsfolk and strangers. Depositional events and monumental constructions stood at opposite ends of the temporal continuum, with deposition having the potential to build up impressive cumulative effects from short-term acts performed by a handful of people, as contrasted to monuments arising out of planned constructions, often involving hundreds of people. Although there would have been overlaps between the forms of depositional events and monumental constructions that took place on small sites and megasites, the range and diversity of these events on megasites would have massively exceeded those on small sites, whether these were public or private events. It is important to remember that all acts of deposition presenced absent people, places and things.

1.3.4 Formal Open Spaces

Open spaces would have been central to the development of megasites as congregational places – the space for the largest meetings of the regional calendar.

Monica Smith (2008) has underlined the significance of open spaces not so much as neutral spaces but spaces sustained to support a wide range of cultural memories at different temporalities, although conflict could also feature in such places. Open spaces were often many times larger than the size of a 'normal' settlement, creating an unprecedented and spectacular venue for visitors from small sites. Unlike formal open spaces such as the agora, forum, plaza, odeon, amphitheatre or hippodrome, there were varied ways by which open spaces on megasites were integrated into the other parts of the site, whether through formal layouts (Trypilla megasites) or less formal areas juxtaposed with dwelling areas and/or public monuments (Valencina de la Concepción). This raises the challenging issue of the number of people in such gatherings.

If we take an arbitrary figure for a large, dense gathering such as the Hadj, the mean value of one person per square metre in an open space of 10 ha results in the improbable total of 100,000 people. The involvement in open-air performances of both participants *and* spectators meant the differentiation of space, whether presenting a scene surrounded by the audience, multi-foci performances more akin to a street festival or craft production with potentially dangerous side-effects (e.g., kiln-firing of pottery). An impossible minimum number for a 10 ha open space would be 10–100 people – a meeting scale more suitable for a small settlement. Another factor links the number of people in a congregation to the number of people involved in its construction. Taking all of these factors into account, a provisional size range of a congregation in a 10 ha open space would have been 100 to 1,000 people, resulting in a density of one to ten people per 100 m^2. This density range should be set against the often extreme size of megasite open spaces, which could cover several hundred hectares.

1.3.5 Performance

Performance is what activated a congregation place – what gave a site its dynamic agency on a massive scale. We propose that such sites were characterised by their *habitus* of performance, which we find is an excellent way of invoking the people so often missing from studies of megasites and who brought the megasite to such dynamic life. The sensory experiences of performances – whether the sounds and smells of smoke or lighting or a dramatic experience – would have been heightened, especially at major megasite events. While many modest, perhaps private performative acts were certainly found on all sites, it was the larger-scale public performances that distinguished the megasites from the rest. What is challenging to gauge is the importance of the intangible cultural heritage in these events – the dancing, singing and chanting (Fig. 7). The larger-scale events featured three types of performance – feasting, deposition (see Section 1.3.3) and processions.

Large-scale feasting has been recognised as a classic means of integrating diverse groups and generating cultural memories, while at the same time raising the social status of its providers (OA/Dietler 2006; OA/Hayden & Villeneuve 2011). In European megasites, the implications of slaughtering a herd animal, whether a caprid or a bovid, were the provision of large quantities of meat for communal feasting (for a bovid, 300–400 kg). Kassabaum (2019) has framed her analysis of feasting with two intersecting axes – group size versus competitive (high-status) – non-competitive/egalitarian (low-status) feasts, noting overlaps between the food and drink consumed in each combination. The primary characteristic of a megasite feast was surely the large-scale, low-status feast in the inner open area.

Processions were one of most important ways for people to meet a wide range of other visitors. While the monuments at certain megasites constituted the end-point of major processions, there were other megasites in which site planning (Trypillia megasites) guided processions or built features (Bil'sk) defined processional route-ways. Major ceremonies forming the start or the finish of the procession would have made a big contribution to the *habitus* of megasite performance.

1.3.6 Congregational Catchments

Catchments require definition to set the megasites in their broad network context and show the scale of links between communities across the landscape. The term 'congregation catchment' indicates regular interaction between the residents at the megasite and others, including visitors, over a certain distance, which varied with each site according to its position in the regional settlement network. We propose a preliminary distinction between an inner zone, with more intensive interaction and the provision of heavier everyday things such as ground stone, salt and potting clay, and an outer zone with less frequent but still potentially signifi-cant interaction, bringing colourful, shiny things such as ornaments, pigments, jadeite, copper daggers, gold bowls or ivory, to the megasites. An important task is to define the spatial boundary between inner and outer zones for each megasite. The overnight visits to intermediate sites by visitors travelling more than 20 km to a megasite consolidated these interaction networks.

Three kinds of evidence can be used to define a congregation catchment: settlement pattern, people and things. Formal modelling of settlement patterns has been used to delineate Trypillia megasite catchments (Nebbia 2020), while Thiessen polygons or informal settlement networks offered more general insights for Bil'sk. Strontium isotope and aDNA analysis of human remains can locate the origins and biographies of buried individuals. However, since strontium isotope analysis cannot detect annual visits of up to three months to the main site from residence elsewhere, the results can indicate only a general catchment for the buried population. We question the assumption that most people buried at a centre derived from the local settlement(s), proposing that some of the deceased were brought from the inner zone and only occasional individuals (or their parts) coming from the outer zone.

Things can act as proxies of exchange and other forms of interaction, as well as the cultural significance of exotica to a megasite. The form of transport used to bring the things to megasites varied through prehistory, with human movement constant and enhanced settlement mobility provided by wheeled transport with cattle or horse traction from the Bronze Age onwards and large sea-going vessels in the Iron Age.

In summary, megasites as congregation places were among the most extraordinary sites in European prehistory – distinguished from smaller, coeval settlements in a range of ways that are well illustrated by the six parameters chosen for study. Nowhere else in the cultural world of any megasite would related kinsfolk meet so many 'strangers' (viz., from the same cultural background) or even 'stranger strangers' (from other, more remote places and times). Such gatherings were understandably rare since a round-trip journey of 200 km was not a simple undertaking. Yet when they happened, the events at megasites defined the life experience of a generation of residents and visitors – bringing transformative scalar benefits and costs.

1.4 Structure of the Element

The structure of this Element is straightforward. Sandwiched between an introductory section and a discussion and summary of the principal findings of the research (Section 7) are five sections in which, with one exception, a general introduction to the period in question precedes a more detailed analysis of a single, representative megasite (Sections 2–6). Six detailed analyses – the mortuary and land use modelling and the construction of 'houses of the dead' at Alsónyék, the chronological analyses of Valencina de la Concepción and the labour studies at Cornești and Bil'sk – are placed in the Online Appendix, together with a more detailed account of the European Iron Age and much of the further reading (references beginning OA/, as in OA/Anderson 1991).

In Section 2, we begin with a recapitulation of a whole class of megasites – the 4th millennium cal BC Trypillia megasites. Since we have already published a detailed study of the Nebelivka megasite (Gaydarska 2020), we offer a comparison of the three largest Trypillia megasites – Taljanki, Nebelivka and Majdanetske.

In Section 3, we go back in time to the 5th millennium cal BC – to the Late Neolithic and Chalcolithic of the Balkans and the Carpathian Basin and the Late Neolithic of Central Europe. Despite a range of potential megasites with evidence for settlement congregations, we have chosen the Lengyel site of

Alsónyék, in south-western Hungary, as an example of a mortuary congregation place that resulted in the largest mortuary complex known in Neolithic Europe.

Our choice of megasite for discussion in Section 4 is Valencina de la Concepción, near Sevilla, in Southern Spain – a site whose precise chronological sequence (3200–2300 cal BC) resulted from its inclusion in the 'ToTL' Project. The size of the complex and the diversity of its finds at Valencina made this an obvious choice when considered in comparison with the smaller megasites and other enclosures of Neolithic and Copper Age Southern Europe, including Italy, southern France and southern Iberia.

In the utterly different world of the European Bronze Age, dominated by small hillforts and peopled by dispersed homestead groups, it is rare to find any megasite at all. Once a landscape marked by mega-forts had been identified in the Carpathian Basin, it was clear that one site stood out from all others in the 2nd millennium cal BC for inclusion in Section 5 – the huge enclosed site of Corneşti.

The final choice of a 1st millennium cal BC, Iron Age megasite for treatment in Section 6 was also surprisingly straightforward, even though the size and complexity of Late Iron Age *oppida* in western and central Europe were well known. Our selection returns us to the Ukraine, where the largest hillfort in Europe was founded at Bil'sk (aka 'Bel'sk') around the time of the earliest Greek colonies on the North Pontic shore. This choice was made particularly easy because of the almost total neglect of the site (a single, three-line mention) in the *Oxford Handbook of the Europen Iron Age* (Haselgrove et al. 2018).

While other localities could undoubtedly have been proposed for inclusion, we are content that each of these five examples constitutes a place that conveys important aspects of the period in question. In other words, these five megasites are not 'representative' of their millennium in a statistical sense but in the cultural sense of a central place whose congregational practices 'represent' the wider regional society in which it is embedded. It is for this reason that we remain confident that this choice of five megasites not only provides a key to understanding the creation and maintenance of the megasites themselves but also helps us to move forward in a broader understanding of European prehistory.

2 Trypillia Megasites, Ukraine

2.1 Introduction

The Trypillia group was but one part of the wider Cucuteni-Trypillia group, whose immense duration of over two millennia (4800–2700 cal BC) was matched only by its extreme size of cca. 250,000km^2 (Videiko 2013; Gaydarska 2020) (Fig. 2). Although there were many shared features of Cucuteni and Trypillia material culture in pottery, figurines and houses, there was a divergence in settlement

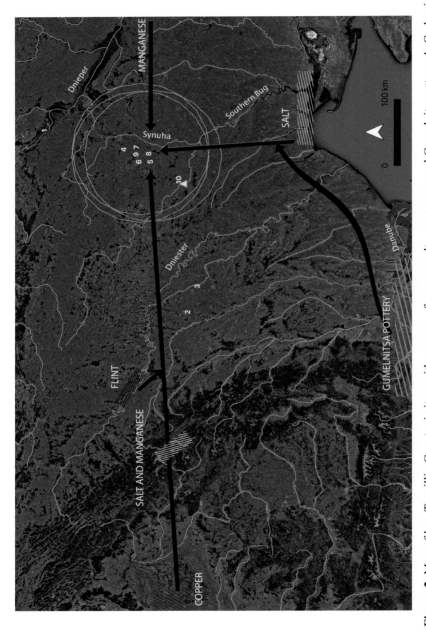

Figure 2 Map of key Trypillia-Cucuteni sites, with sources of copper, salt, manganese and Gumelniţa pottery: 1. Grebeni; 2. Stolniceni; 3. Petreni; 4. Vesely Kut; 5. Apolianka; 6. Dobrovody; 7. Maidanetske; 8. Nebelivka; 9. Taljanki; 10. Haivoron graphite (source: M. Nebbia and Nebelivka Project)

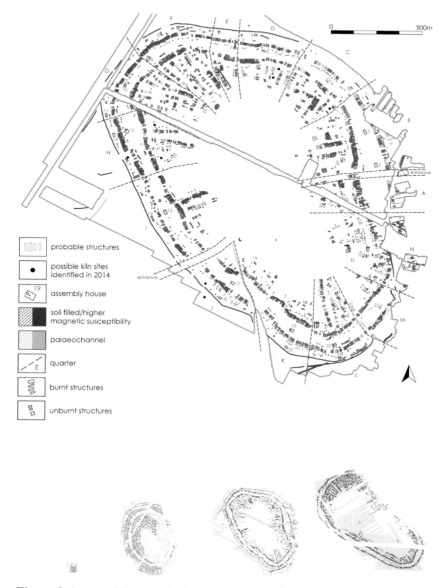

Figure 3 (upper) Plan of Nebelivka + Quarters; (lower) plan showing size of Grebeni relative to megasites (source: authors)

trajectories between the two groups, with Cucuteni sites rarely covering more than a few hectares but with Trypillia sites growing to 10 ha in Phase A, 100 ha in Phase BI and 236 ha in Phase BII (Fig. 3). Sites of 100 ha or more have been dubbed 'megasites' (Chapman et al. 2014), the largest of which (the Phase CI Taljanki)

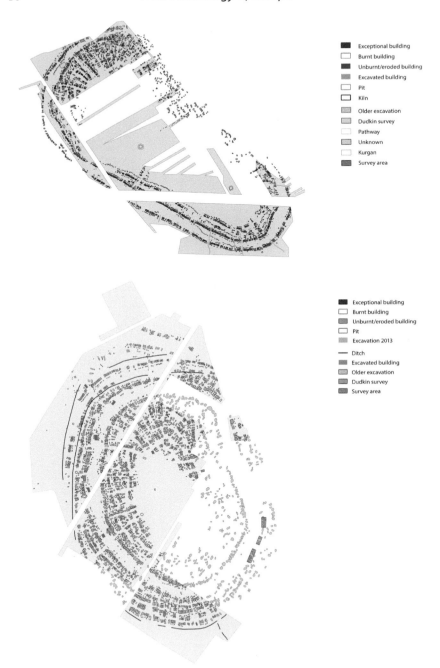

Figure 4 (upper) Plan of Taljanki;
(lower) plan of Maidanetske (source: OA/Rassmann et al. 2014, figs. 3.1a and 22a)

reached 320 ha (OA/Rassmann et al. 2014) (Fig. 4). The megasites clustered in the interfluves between the Southern Bug and Dnieper rivers, with outliers to the east and west.

Although Trypillia settlements were discovered at the turn of the 19th century (OA/Khvoika 1901), megasites were not identified until the 'first methodological revolution' of the 1960s–1970s, when aerial reconnaissance revealed the complex plans of hundreds of burnt houses, which, on excavation, were found associated with Trypillia pottery (Videiko 2013). After forty years of mostly house excavation, the 'second methodological revolution' was initiated in the late 2000s, with international teams using remote sensing, AMS dating and a battery of palaeo-environmental techniques to access new information (Chapman et al. 2014; Müller et al. 2016). The primary focus of the more precise geophysical investigations remained megasite plans (Figs. 3–4), still dominated by burnt houses but also including new features such as unburnt houses, communal buildings termed 'Assembly Houses', pits, industrial structures and pathways. Supra-household configurations showed two levels of site structure – Neighbourhoods comprising three to twenty-seven houses and Quarters comprising five to eighteen Neighbourhoods. The new plans also showed marked architectural variability, suggesting a bottom-up approach to planning that had hitherto been overlooked.

However, these methodological breakthroughs were necessary but insufficient advances to gain a deeper understanding of megasite communities, not least to answer the question of urban status. Gaydarska (OA/2016; 2020, chapter 6.3) developed a relational approach to megasites through the structured comparison of the Nebelivka megasite with the small Trypillia settlement of Grebeni – an approach that provides the framework for this Element (see Section 1) (Fig. 2). In a later study, a detailed comparison of the six parameters used in this Element was made for the three Trypillia megasites of Taljanki, Nebelivka and Maidanetske (Gaydarska & Chapman 2021) (Figs. 3–4). The remainder of this section summarises the main points made in this recent research on the congregational significance of the Trypillia megasites.

2.1.1 Scale

The size of the majority of Trypillia sites in each Phase was 10 ha or less (Nebbia 2020) – a reminder that small community size and limited site size were central to the Trypillia *habitus*. The appearance of megasites was utterly unexpected for their communities, with the increase in scale proving transformative on all levels. This was as true for the number of houses constructed and burnt each year as it was for the building and moving of Assembly Houses from one Neighbourhood to another. It was also true for the construction of the largest Assembly House at

Figure 5 (upper) Reconstruction of Nebelivka mega-structure
(source: C. Unwin and Nebelivka Project); (lower) House-burning,
Nebelivka (source: Nebelivka Project Archive)

Nebelivka – the so-called Mega-structure (Fig. 5) – with its great size matched only by the massive assemblage of mostly fragmented vessels deposited before its final burning. And it was also true for the large number of Quarters and Neighbourhoods planned for Nebelivka – each Quarter larger than a 'normal' small Trypillia settlement site and each Neighbourhood the living space for the visitors from a single small settlement.

2.1.2 Temporality

The insight from a global study of 'Anomalous Giants' that many megasites were occupied temporally or on a seasonal basis (Fletcher 2019) stimulated a consideration of the multiple temporalities present on Trypillia megasites. Each of the three models presented to explain the development and persistence of Nebelivka as a place of major inter-regional gatherings (Gaydarska 2020, chapter 6.1.3) featured different temporalities. The 'Distributed Governance' model proposed a permanent resident population, with annual changes in logistical support between local communities (OA/Gaydarska 2021); the 'Assembly' model combined a massive one-month congregation each year with a small permanent population of megasite 'Guardians' (OA/Nebbia et al. 2018); while the 'Pilgrimage' model, also featuring the Guardians, focussed on a seven–month long pilgrimage season in which pilgrims would spend one month at the centre (OA/Chapman & Gaydarska 2019). There was a marked contrast in temporality between the dwelling part of megasites, with the longer-term continuities reinforced by the one- or two-storey houses, and the inner open area, defined by the punctuated temporality typical of congregational practices.

2.1.3 Deposition and Monumentality

If the core of Trypillia archaeology is the selective deposition and fragmentation of objects, deposition lies at the heart of punctuated temporality. The variability of megasite deposition concerns the context of the event – whether private (in a house) or public (in a large pit or the site's perimeter ditch) – as much as its timing (inside a house before burning or placed on the top of the burnt remains) and the scale of the practice, which ranged from placing fragments of ten vessels in a pit to the filling of the largest Assembly House at Nebelivka (Fig. 5) with parts of 332 vessels before the two-stage burning of the structure. Participation in the deposition event revealed contrasts in relations between persons and households, with deposited objects presencing other places, other persons and other times.

The experience of monumentality varied with perspective, whether witnessing the sounds, smells and sight of a megasite in its entirety from a neighbouring hill or the local appreciation of a ceremony such as a procession towards an Assembly House or a two-storey dwelling house in flames. The cumulative growth of minor mortuary landmarks such as the memory mounds (Fig. 6) transformed Nebelivka from a place of the living into a meeting place for the living and the ancestors.

2.1.4 Open Spaces

The paradox at the heart of the vast open areas at the centre of Trypillia megasites is that the areas with potentially the most significant interaction have left the least evidence for such social practices. The impressive size of these open areas (Figs. 3–4) can be related to two factors. Their multiple functions could have included the corralling of animals, more stationary specialised production (like pottery) but also pop-up crafts (like flint knapping) at times of craft-fairs, as well as a place for meetings, rituals, ceremonies, games, performances, competitions, feasts, debates, gossiping, public display, the exchange of goods, ideas, skills and know-how, singing, dancing, commemoration, grieving, celebrating and match-making – all on an unprecedented scale. Some activities would have involved spectators and participants, others would have consisted just of participants. Such functional complexity would

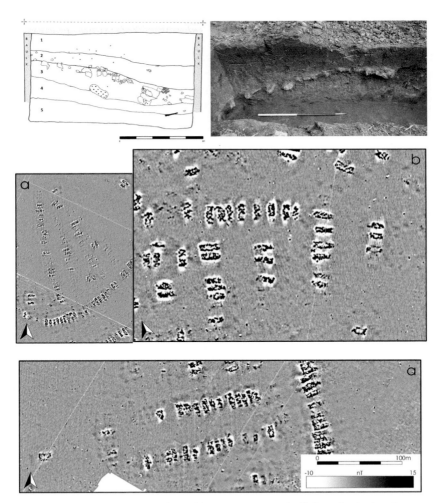

Figure 6 Memory mounds and inner streets, Nebelivka: clockwise from upper left: memory mound, TP 24/4; memory mound, TP 22/4; square and blocking streets, Quarter G; parallel inner radial streets with blocking street, Quarter B; converging inner radial streets, Quarter L
(source: Nebelivka Project Archive)

have required large spaces, while there was a recursive relationship between large areas and large congregations (Smith 2008). The plans of each of the three major megasites reveal different relationships between the open congregational zone and the estimated site population. The rationale behind the open spaces at Nebelivka and Taljanki would have included large numbers of both visitors and locals, while, at Maidanetske, the cumulative reduction of the inner open area would have restricted use to either all the residents with no visitors or special residents with particular visitors.

2.1.5 Performance

Performance was an essential part of the Trypillia *habitus*, closely related as it was to the timemarks of the social calendar. What differentiated megasite performance from those at smaller sites was the significance of major ceremonies. The temporality of performance included three stages – preparations, the performance itself and the incorporation into social memory. These timemarks took four principal forms: house-burning, feasting, other kinds of deposition and processions. As the Nebelivka Project discovered during their experimental house-burning (OA/Gaydarska et al. 2019), the stunning visual effects of house conflagrations (Fig. 5) were amongst the most memorable events of the calendar, not diminished by their regularity and notable for the unique scale of Assembly House burning. All four forms of feasting as delineated in Kassabaum's (2019) feasting typology could be identified at Nebelivka through the varied form and scale of animal bone deposition. Object deposition formed the centrepiece of hundreds of other depositional performances in all the main megasite contexts. The well-established principles of megasite planning, including the space between the two principal house circuits as well as the parallel inner radial streets leading into the inner open area (Fig. 6), conformed closely to the performance of processions into and around the megasite (Fig. 7).

2.1.6 Congregational Catchment

The interpretation of a congregational catchment relates to the people visiting the megasite and the objects that arrived there. In view of the absence of human burials at megasites, Marco Nebbia (2020) has developed formal settlement modelling to demonstrate that the majority of megasite interactions took place in up to a 100 km radius. In the sense that the movement of people living more than 15–20 km from a megasite meant overnight stays at smaller settlements, the congregation process led to a consolidation of social relations within the catchment.

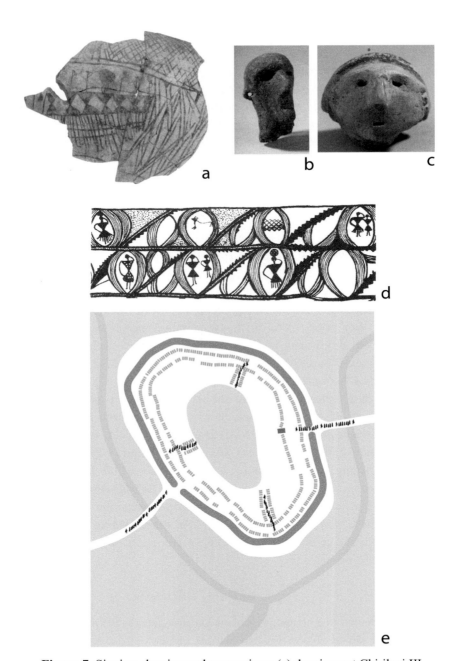

Figure 7 Singing, dancing and processions: (a) dancing pot Chirileni III
(Gaydarska & Chapman 2021, fig. 2.6a, based upon OA/Monah 2016, fig. 268/1);
(b) Kolomiishchina singing figurines (Gaydarska & Chapman 2021, fig. 2.6b,
based upon Ciuk 2008, p. 227); (c) singing figurine, Maidanetske (Gaydarska &
Chapman 2021, fig. 2.6c, based upon OA/Ciuk 2008, p. 215); (d) dancing scene,
Brânzeni (Gaydarska & Chapman 2021, fig. 2.6d, based upon OA/Monah 2016,
fig. 249/3); (e) Nebelivka procession (source: C. Unwin & Nebelivka Project)

Early Trypillia communities were connected to the jadeite network linking the French Alps and Eastern Europe, with two axes known from dated contexts: Slobidka – Zahidna (Phase AIII) and Berezivka (Phase BI) (OA/ Pétrequin et al. 2017). In the later megasite phase, no more jadeite is known but small quantities of copper, gold, salt, chipped stone and manganese pigment (Fig. 8) came from beyond the 100 km catchment in two stages. First, the exotics were brought into the catchment, from which local visitors brought them to megasites. Later, with the expansion in the fame of congregations, long-distance specialists (*sensu* OA/Helms 1988) had the opportunity to bring exotics directly to the megasites. Such exotics were one of the many attractions for visitors to megasites; no wonder visitors took them home instead of depositing them at the megasite.

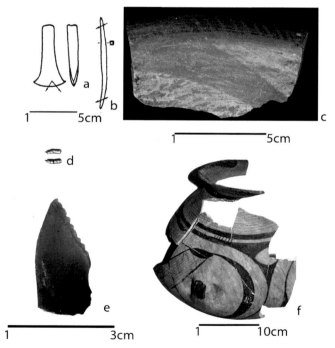

Figure 8 Exotics at megasites: (a) copper axe, Maidanetske (source: OA/ Ryndina 1998, Ris. 66/6, re-drawn by Lauren Woodard); (b) copper awl, Taljanki (source: OA/Ryndina 1998, Ris. 66/12, re-drawn by Lauren Woodard); (c) Nebelivka graphite-painted dish with internally thickened rim; (d) Nebelivka gold ornament (7 x 3 mm); (e) Prut – Dniester flint, TP 19/2; (f) Nebelivka painted vessel (manganese) TP 1/3 (source for (c)–(f): Nebelivka Project Archive)

2.2 Conclusion

Trypillia megasites can be considered as an exemplar of congregation sites for European prehistory, with many of the six variables discussed here appropriate to an analysis of later potential megasites. One of the outstanding features of Trypillia megasites was the combination of a major dwelling zone with a massive open congregation area. This combination shows that the supposed mutual exclusivity between dwelling and ritual/deposition is a false dichotomy. There is also no contradiction between a congregation centre and a site of urban status, since the former influenced all the performances of the latter.

3 Neolithic and Copper Age Sites in the Balkans and Central Europe

3.1 Introduction

The Balkans and Central Europe resemble the Cucuteni-Trypillia distribution in the domination of their Neolithic archaeology by settlement remains. The mortuary domain was relatively minor in most areas and, until the Fall of the Berlin Wall opened up the floodgates of remote sensing in these regions, there were relatively few known public monuments, except for the Late Neolithic *Hohensiedlungen* (hill-top sites) and *Rondels* (circular enclosures) of Central Europe (OA/Petrasch 2015). By the 2020s, our understanding of the Neolithic landscapes of Hungary and South East Europe has been transformed by the discovery of large numbers of enclosures, some built in combination with Balkan site types such as tells. However, even using the relational approach to site size and scale, we can identify relatively few megasites in regions where nucleated settlements are common (Table 1). Why is it that there were so few megasites in such settlement-rich landscapes?

A well-known trait of Neolithic lifeways is a reduction in mobility, whose reduction in direct access to 'resources' was mitigated by an increase in exchange practices between more settled places. This created a new form of the Palaeolithic problem of the 'absence' of the vast majority of people known by a community, because they were living elsewhere. One common Neolithic response in increasingly permanent communities was the creation of seasonal meeting places.

In the Earlier Neolithic (6300–5300 BC), we can distinguish between tell landscapes in North Macedonia and Bulgaria and landscapes dominated by 'flat' sites (Romania, Central Balkans, Hungary) (OA/Chapman 2020a) (Fig. 9).

Table 1 Large Neolithic settlement sites and megasites in South-East and Central Europe

Name and Region	Date	Maximum Size (Ha)	Principal Features	ReferEnce
Drenovac, Serbia (Fig. 10a)	6th–5th mill. BC	40 ha	Large multi-layer, polyfocal open Vinča site after long-lasting Starčevo occupation	OA/Perić & Miletić 2020
Selevac, Serbia	5th mill. BC	53 ha	Open multi-layer Vinča settlement	OA/Tringham & Krstić 1990
Borđoš, Serbia	Early 5th mill. BC	38 ha	Polyfocal Vinča-Tisza complex with a tell and small *Rondel* replaced by a larger enclosure with a central mound	OA/Hofmann et al. 2019
Csőszhalom, Hungary (Fig. 11)	4850–4500 BC	63 ha	Eponymous polyfocal complex with one tell enclosed by multiple ditches, a smaller enclosure and a large horizontal settlement	OA/Raczky 2018
Szeghalom, Hungary	Mid-5th mill. BC	70 ha	Polyfocal Tisza complex with a tell and a large horizontal flat site with many house clusters	OA/Parkinson et al. 2017
Alsónyék, Hungary (Fig. 14)	5800–4400 BC	50 ha	See Section 3.2.	OA/Rassmann et al. 2020
Zengővárkóny Hungary	5th mill. BC	45 ha	Open Lengyel settlement defined by clusters of houses and graves, with a *Rondel* in the middle of the settlement	Bertók & Gáti 2014
Urmitz, Germany (Fig. 12)	4th mill BC	100–120 ha	Ditched and palisaded Late Neolithic enclosure of semi-circular form	OA/Boelicke 1976/7
Wiesbaden-Schierstein, Germany (Fig. 12)	4th mill. BC	100 ha	Ditched and palisaded Late Neolithic enclosure of semi-circular form	OA/Petrasch 2015

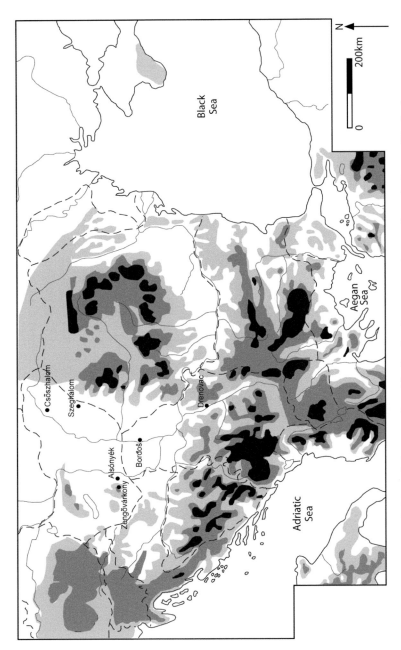

Figure 9 Map of sites mentioned in Section 3 (source: authors, re-drawn by Lauren Woodard)

The Bulgarian tells are a classic example of what we have discussed as segmentary societies (see Section 1.2) – mostly small settlements defined by often low mounds, with site populations of 50–75 people. The mating networks required for long-term viability would have needed the participation of 10–12 tells. With high densities of houses on the tell, 'off-tell' meeting places were the obvious solution but there is little tradition of excavating away from the tell in these countries. One of the few Earlier Neolithic enclosures in a tell-dominated landscape was at Yabulkovo, in South Bulgaria (OA/Roodenberg et al. 2014) (here Fig. 10a) – a triple-ditched enclosure with deposition in pits in the central area.

In the non-tell world of the Starčevo – Körös – Criş groups, settlement varied between one-house sites, hamlets and villages (OA/Chapman 2008). Village sites such as Alsónyék, in Hungary, Leţ, in Romania or Galovo in Croatia, may have included meeting places within their settlement but these are not obvious. This leaves enclosed sites such as Cârcea, in South West Romania, as a potential congregation place.

In the Later Neolithic (5300–4600 BC), amidst rising regional settlement densities and the expansion of tell lifeways, there was an increased diversity of site types and sizes, with larger sites showing a greater variety of combinations of site elements such as the mound, the horizontal settlement, the *Rondel* and the enclosure (Chapman 2020, chapter 5). But the basic settlement unit reproducing segmentary societies was the small tell or flat site of <2 ha area with a population of <100 people. This was true of most phases of the Karanovo sequence in South Bulgaria, with the exception of phase IV, when most people lived on flat sites and created meeting places characterised by extensive deposition of ordinary day-to-day objects in pits.

In places where increased sedentism had led to greater population nucleation (Table 1), the concentration of so many people perhaps meant that off-site assembly places were not necessary. However, the geophysical plots of sites such as Drenovac (Fig. 10b), Pločnik and Belovode show few signs of a meeting place within the settlement. It should be noted that the largest Vinča sites were not as big as proposed earlier (OA/Chapman 1981). On the basis of new fieldwork, the 100 ha size of Potporanj refers to an area of 1 sq km where settlement was in fact highly discontinuous; equally, the 80 ha size of Selevac can be revised downwards to 53 ha and the 65 ha of Turdaş to 23 ha. By contrast, Csőszhalom included two special assembly foci – a tell and an enclosure – within a large horizontal

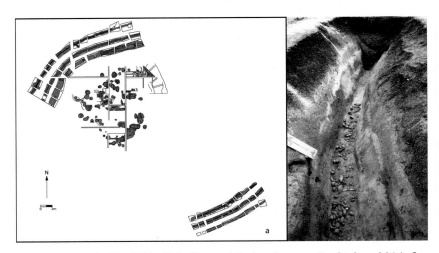

Figure 10 Early Neolithic Yabulkovo: (a) plan (source: Leshtakov 2014, fig. 77, re-drawn by Lauren Woodard) and ditch B1 (source: Petrova 2014, fig. 3.7); (b) geophysical plan of Drenovac (K. Rassmann)

settlement (Fig. 11). Elsewhere, combinations of a tell within, or adjacent to, an enclosure at sites such as Uivar, Szeghalom and Bordjoš illustrates how meeting places could be incorporated into site plans.

In Transdanubia and Croatia, a far higher density of enclosed sites was found in the Sopot and Lengyel groups than in the Central Balkans. Two sets of enclosures are known – the Djakovo (OA/Šošić-Klindžić et al. 2019) and Szemely (Bertók & Gáti 2014) groups, each with remarkably different enclosure morphologies. In the former, the site of Tomašanci comprises five separate small Sopot enclosures, while the largest site of Gorjani – Kremenjača – revealed multiple dwelling features within three concentric ditches. By contrast, most of the enclosures in the Szemely group were *Rondels* of widely differing complexity (Fig. 13). The presence of an enclosure or an empty space at the centre of several Sopot settlements suggests regular on-site assembly places. An unusual combination concerns the creation of a *Rondel* in the middle of the Lengyel settlement site of Zengővárkóny, with its clusters of houses and burials. This site forms a major contrast to Alsónyék, which lacks a *Rondel* (see Section 3.2). A settlement that does not obviously fit these Central Balkan-Carpathian patterns is Iclod, in Transylvania, with its so far unique combination of enclosure, settlement remains and mortuary zone.

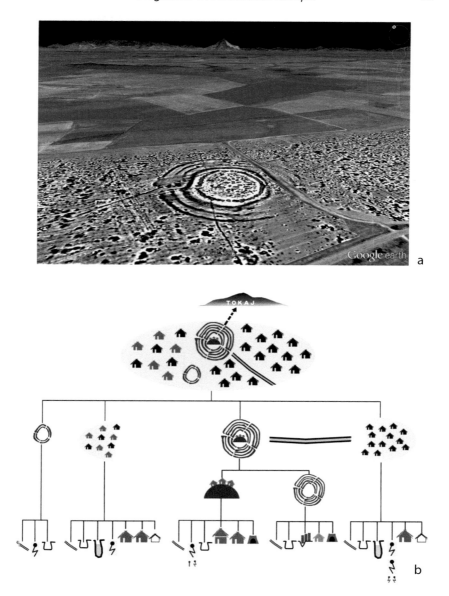

Figure 11 Plan of the Csőszhalom complex (source: OA/Raczky 2018, fig. 3.1)

The emergence of cemeteries in the late 6th millennium cal BC created an alternative domain for the negotiation of ancestral links to that of the well-developed domestic domain (Chapman 2020, chapter 6). Cemeteries were rare until c. 4800 cal BC, even though large complexes such as

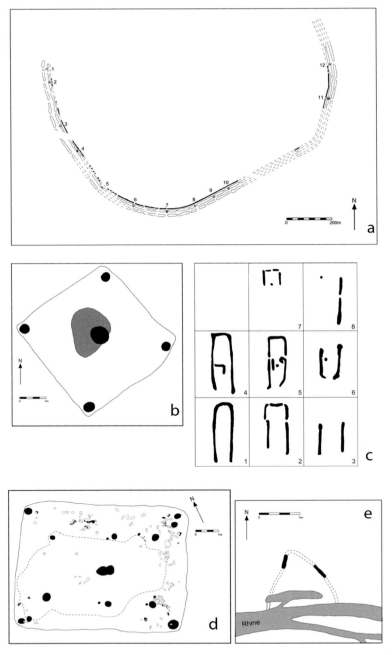

Figure 12 (a) Plan of Urmitz; (b) bastions at gates, Urmitz; (c) Hut 1, Urmitz;
(d) Hut 6, Urmitz; (e) plan of Wiesbaden – Schierstein (source: OA/Boelicke,
U. 1976/7, figs.1.1, 2.2–2.3, 2.6 and 6.7/4: re-drawn by Lauren Woodard)

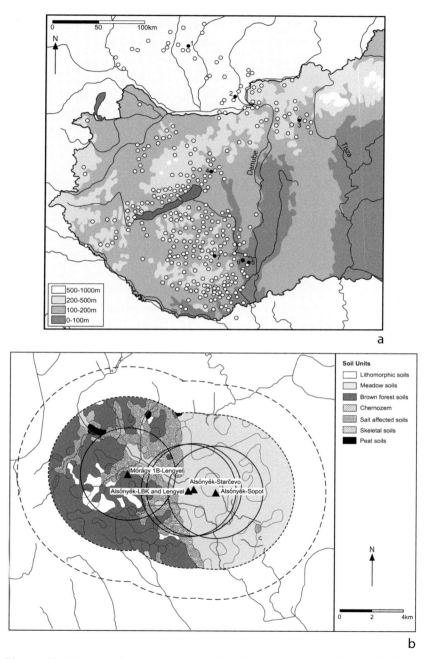

Figure 13 (a) Lengyel sites in the Carpathian Basin (source: OA/Scharl 2016, fig. 2.4), with enclosed sites in Co. Baranya (source: Bertók & Gàti 2014, II.90) (combined and re-drawn by Lauren Woodard); (b) Soil environment of Alsónyék and Mórágy (source: Depaermentier et al. 2020, fig. 2.1b, re-drawn by Lauren Woodard)

Cernica (Romania), with c. 378 burials, were known from early on. The only region with consistent cemetery usage from 5300 cal BC onwards was the Western Black Sea coast (Hamangia group). This formed the basis for exceptional cemeteries such as Varna, with the world's first concentration of gold objects (OA/Ivanov & Avramova 2000), and Durankulak – until Alsónyék, the largest aggregation of burials in South East Europe (OA/ Todorova 2002). Alongside cemeteries of 30–100 burials, there were rare instances of mortuary congregations, such as the sample of over 10,000 bones (human and animal) deposited in four pits at Alba Iulia – Lumea Noua, representing over 100 human individuals whose bones were brought from other sites for central burial (OA/Gligor 2009). Elsewhere, in the Lengyel group, clusters of burials lay close to sets of houses in a pattern fundamentally different from the small- to medium-size cemeteries of the East Balkans and reaching 368 burials at sites such as Zengővárkóny (OA/ Dombay 1960).

The general conclusions are that, for the Earlier Neolithic, there were few examples of settlements with obvious meeting places and even fewer special and separate meeting places. For the Later Neolithic, meeting places were often defined within the overall boundaries of large sites, even if the site was dominated by everyday dwelling. The exceptions were Karanovo phase IV pit sites and sites in any region with a high proportion of small dispersed settlements.

The largest sites in the Balkan-Carpathian regions were between twenty and forty times as large as the usual small (<2 ha) dispersed segmented settlement. There was undoubtedly an up-scaling factor in site practices at these larger settlements, which nonetheless seemed to fall below the threshold of megasites. Many of these long-lasting Balkan settlements formed key nodes in stable exchange and marriage networks, perhaps displacing the need for even larger sites. If the Trypillia megasites emerged in the context of agro-pastoral frontier conditions during the eastwards Trypillia expansion (see Section 2), we should perhaps look for megasites in the initial Neolithic expansion into South East Europe. However, the restriction of the site sizes during the earliest farming expansion to a tenth smaller than those of the Early Trypillia sites meant a far lower starting point for site growth, leading to the absence of megasites in the Balkan Early Neolithic. The longer-lived cemeteries, with their hundreds of bodies, offered an alternative ancestral focus to that of the long-lived tells and flat sites.

Further north and west, settlements of the Early Neolithic group termed the *Linearbandkeramik* (or LBK) spread as far as the North Sea and into the Paris

Basin (Bickle & Whittle 2013). As with the first farmers of the Balkans, LBK sites ranged from single-house sites and hamlets to villages. There is currently little evidence for special meeting places in this group, with the exception of the mortuary congregation at the Late LBK Herxheim enclosure (OA/Chapman et al., in press). However, the increased intensity of enclosure, which had already started in the LBK, was a major characteristic of the Late Neolithic, ranging from small *Rondels* to the two megasite enclosures of Urmitz and Wiesbaden – Schierstein, in the Rhein valley – both c. 100–120 ha in size. Although sharing many constructional and depositional details with Michelsberg and other North European enclosures, these two sites appear to form a class of their own (OA/Petrasch 2015).

Both sites share a semi-circular enclosure form, with ditches 2.5 km long at Urmitz (Fig. 12) and 1.5 km long at Wiesbaden (Fig. 12). Some of the multiple causeways spaced roughly every 100 m at Urmitz had complex entrance-works (OA/Boelicke 1976/7) (here Fig. 12 inset). While there was frequent deposition of pottery in the ditches at both sites, with burials in the ditches at Urmitz, Wiesbaden showed a wider range of deposition in the interior than Urmitz, with some evidence for on-site antler-working and flint-knapping. Small rectangular houses were found in the interior at Urmitz alongside over 75 pits. No explanation has been provided for the extreme size of these enclosures, although Gronenborn et al. (OA/2020) have proposed links between Michelsberg enclosures, local hierarchies and the exchange of salt and jadeite axes. While Gronenborn (p.c., February 2021) has confirmed the rarity of coeval sites in the Urmitz catchment, an explanation of congregation sites should be considered for Urmitz and Wiesbaden – Schierstein.

3.2 Alsónyék: A Mortuary Congregation Site?

Alsónyék-Bátaszék is located in Transdanubia in modern-day Hungary and associated with several Neolithic cultural groups (Starčevo, LBK, Sopot and Lengyel). The site was excavated in advance of the M6 motorway in 2006–9 and produced 15,000 features (Osztás et al. 2016a) (Fig. 14). It is an extraordinary site on five grounds. It is the longest-lived flat site in the European Neolithic, with over a millennium of uninterrupted occupation (5350 cal BC to 4300 cal BC) that is comparable only to tells. Its estimated size of c. 50 ha is the largest known Lengyel occupation. Its 2,300+ Lengyel graves constitute an unparalleled burial phenomenon. It was extensively excavated over an area of 25 ha, showing huge numbers of houses, burials, pits and pit-complexes and over 500,000 sherds. Finally, the site benefits from exemplary applications of best practice in archaeological science (e.g. Bayliss et. al 2016; Depaermentier et al. 2020a, 2020b). Almost every aspect of

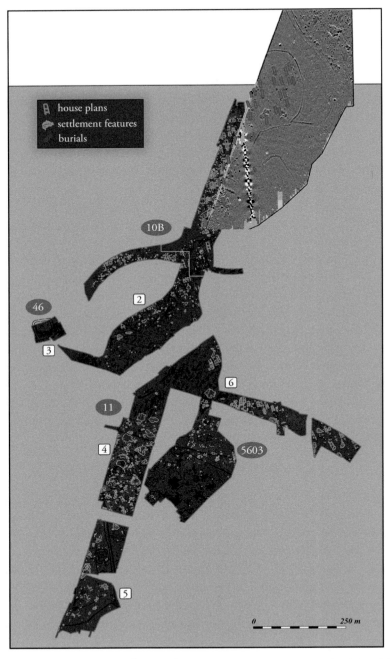

Figure 14 Plan of Alsónyék complex (source: Osztás et al. 2016a, fig. 2.6 and OA/
Rassmann 2020, fig. 4.8, with additions by Lauren Woodard)

this amazing site has important implications for our understanding of cultural developments in Western Hungary. There is an ongoing publication programme of the resultant massive corpus of data and analysis, with some crucial results already published (Bánffy et al. 2016). We concentrate here only on the published data on the Lengyel occupation phase, with its 122 houses and over 2,300 burials, representing 90 per cent of all Alsónyék graves.

The unprecedented number of burials led to the hypothesis of an equally vast 'coalescent community' living at Alsónyék (Bánffy et al. 2016). Details about our insights on this model and the pathway to the alternative suggestion of mortuary congregation are provided online (Online Appendix I). Our starting point is that the relationship between burial and settlement is not straightforward, as burial preceded the start of dwelling activities and ceased before the end of the Lengyel settlement. This suggests that it is the huge concentration of *burials* that defines this site. In short, instead of the emergence of a coalescent community of more than 2,000 people over fifty years, we see a process of nucleation of half that number of people – still unprecedented in the Lengyel context – only part of whom were buried in Alsónyék alongside people who were brought to Alsónyék as their final resting place. It is possible that such a burial tradition started in the Sopot period, which may have overlapped with the first Lengyel burials; what is certain is that the earliest Lengyel burials were made without accompanying dwelling practices (Osztás et al. 2016b: 223). Thus the main attraction for the initial dwelling and subsequent nucleation was the increasing importance of Alsónyék as an ancestral mortuary space whose cumulative burials emphasised place-value in the way that repeated dwelling did on tells. Alsónyék's advantage over other places was to provide a cohesive, rather than a competitive, space for the display, negotiation and reproduction of social identities at both the local and regional levels.

3.2.1 Scale

Hardly anyone will disagree that, with its 2,359 Lengyel graves, Alsónyék dwarfs any earlier or later practice of the cumulative deposition of dead bodies, which is a more complex social practice than the body-part mobility attested at Herxheim (OA/Chapman et al. in press) or Lumea Nouă (OA/Gligor 2009). It represents more than a six-fold increase from the next largest cemetery (the 368 burials at Zengővárkóny) and it is more than twenty times larger than the neighbouring Mórágy cemetery, with 109 graves (OA/Regenye et al. 2020). There can be no doubt that Alsónyék reveals a key long-term social practice that cannot be explained simply as a by-product of increased population size. Although population growth has certainly played a role, the long duration of burial beyond the nucleation peak suggests that burying rather than living defined the long-term mortuary congregation over 250–300 years.

3.2.2 Temporality

Although 250–300 years is not necessarily an unusual cemetery duration, it is certainly unusual to bury more than 2,000 people in this period. The average annual rate would have been eight–nine burials, meaning that every snow-free month saw at least one burial, which in itself is far higher than at most other prehistoric cemeteries. However, burials clearly did not occur at an even pace, with episodes of intensive activity interspersed with regular burials. Table 2 shows that the tempo of burial in Alsónyék, regardless of how much of the site has been excavated, is higher than all other cemeteries where burial rate has been determined. The estimation of per annum burials (for algorithm, see Online Appendix I) reaches high figures for each subsite (10B – estimated range of 9–15; 11–4.2; 5603–2.3). The total of fifteen to twenty burials per annum represents the burial of between one-third and one-half of the forty Alsónyék inhabitants who died in one year per 1,000 population – a burial intensity not witnessed thus far in the European Neolithic or Chalcolithic. If this indeed was the case, there is an urgent need to explain the origins of these new and extensive 'rights to burial' and their disappearance. The explanation of such a high burial rate that we propose is that some of the deceased were brought from other sites to Alsónyék for burial. Whether people were dying at Alsónyék or their bodies were brought to the centre, or both, the nucleation peak either side of 4700 cal BC would have seen two–three burials per month for the entire fifty-year period. This calendar of intensive mortuary practices would have had massive social implications, not least huge emotional effects on those living at Alsónyék. The intense tempo of mortuary acts diverged from the steadier temporality of the house clusters. At the same time, this intensive burial programme created cumulative long-term ties between those settlements sending their deceased to Alsónyék and the heterogeneous totality of visitors, reinforcing its place as a major centre for regional ancestors. It is the cumulative concentration of ancestors in huge numbers that created for Alsónyék a special status among the living, the newly dead and the ancestors. These relations formed the lynch-pin of the Lengyel social world, in which identities and memories were co-shaped in a place of increasing long-term significance.

3.2.3 Deposition and Monumentality

Alsónyék strongly evoked the power of cultural memory as a driver and attractor through the maintenance and persistence of depositional practices.

Table 2 Estimated burial rate for various Lengyel cemeteries (source: authors)

Cemetery	Estimated % of Cemetery Excavated	Maximum Burial Rate (Burials/Duration)	Minimum Burial Rate (Burials/Duration)	Estimated Burial Rate (+/-) per annum
Villánykövesd	100 per cent	28 burials/1 year	28 burials/295 years	14 burials each year (14 ± 7)
Villánykövesd	33 per cent	85 burials/1 year	85 burials/295 years	42–43 burials each year (43 ± 21)
Villánykövesd	25 per cent	112 burials/1 year	112 burials/295 years	56 burials each year (56 ± 28)
Mórágy	100 per cent	108 burials/140 years	108 burials/295 years	1 burial every 2 years (0.6 ± 0.1)
Mórágy	33 per cent	327 burials/140 years	327 burials/295 years	1–2 burials each year (1.7 ± 0.3)
Mórágy	25 per cent	432 burials/140 years	432 burials/295 years	2 burials each year (2.3 ± 0.4)
Zengővárkony	100 per cent	368 burials/190 years	368 burials/385 years	1 or 2 burials each year (1.5 ± 0.3)
Zengővárkony	33 per cent	1,115 burials/190 years	1,115 burials/385 years	9 burials every 2 years (4.4 ± 0.7)
Zengővárkony	25 per cent	1,472 burials/190 years	1,472 burials/385 years	Up to 6 burials each year (5.8 ± 1)
Veszprém	100 per cent	8 burials/45 years	8 burials/325 years	1 burial every 10 years (0.1 ± 0.04)
Veszprém	33 per cent	24 burials/45 years	24 burials/325 years	1 burial every 3–4 years (0.3 ± 0.11)
Veszprém	25 per cent	32 burials/45 years	32 burials/325 years	1 burial every 2–3 years (0.4 ± 0.2)
Svodín	100 per cent	111 burials/1 year	111 burials/165 years	56 burials each year (56 ± 27)
Svodín	33 per cent	336 burials/1 year	336 burials/165 years	169 burials each year (169 ± 83.5)
Svodín	25 per cent	444 burials/1 year	444 burials/165 years	225 burials each year (225 ± 109)
Friebritz	100 per cent	10 burials/10 years	10 burials/330 years	1 burial every 2 years (0.5 ± 0.2)

Table 2 (cont.)

Cemetery	Estimated % of Cemetery Excavated	Maximum Burial Rate (Burials/Duration)	Minimum Burial Rate (Burials/Duration)	Estimated Burial Rate (+/-) per annum
Friebritz	33 per cent	30 burials/10 years	30 burials/330 years	1 or 2 burials each year (1.6 ± 0.7)
Friebritz	25 per cent	40 burials/10 years	40 burials/330 years	2 burials each year (2.1 ± 1)
Alsónyék 10B	100 per cent	862 burials/1 year	862 burials/95 years	435 burials each year (435 ± 213)
Alsónyék 10B	33 per cent	2,612 burials/1 year	2,612 burials/95 years	1,320 burials each year (1320 ± 641)
Alsónyék 10B	25 per cent	3,448 burials/1 year	3,448 burials/95 years	2,069 burials each year ($2,069 \pm 853$)
Alsónyék 11	100 per cent	735 burials/120 years	735 burials/325 years	4 burials each year (4.2 ± 1)
Alsónyék 11	33 per cent	2,227 burials/120 years	2,227 burials/325 years	Up to 13 burials each year (12.7 ± 3)
Alsónyék 11	25 per cent	2,940 burials/120 years	2,940 burials/325 years	17 burials each year (16.8 ± 4)
Alsónyék 5603	100 per cent	625 burials/215 years	625 burials/355 years	7 burial every 3 years (2.3 ± 0.3)
Alsónyék 5603	33 per cent	1,893 burials/215 years	1,893 burials/355 years	7 burials each year (7 ± 1)
Alsónyék 5603	25 per cent	2,500 burials/215 years	2,500 burials/355 years	9 burials each year (9.3 ± 1)

The extensive flat site was indeed developed on flat terrain but the site flatness was broken up by the silhouettes of the dramatic houses of the dead and the imposing houses of the living.

The 'houses of the dead' represented by the graves with four large post-holes are so far unique to Alsónyék in the Lengyel group (Zalai-Gaál et al. 2012). Our reconstruction shows the above-ground height of the posts based upon post-hole shape, depth and width (Fig. 15: for modelling of post sizes, see Online Appendix I/2). These houses of the dead, reconstructed as roofed but not walled above-ground structures, were first built in the early decades of the complex, well before the start of the mortuary peak c. 4725 cal BC. At least six houses of the dead were erected before the burial peak in Grave Group 56 – a major site feature forming a visual cluster not unlike a mortuary hamlet. Such early clusters of burials perhaps presenced the living houses on sites whose deceased made their final journey to Alsónyék. Many such houses would have lived for over a century before the timbers rotted and they too joined the world of the ancestors.

The houses of the living formed impressive groups of dwellings dispersed across the site. Their much larger size and their clustering gave them a visual prominence over the houses of the dead that belied the priority of the mortuary domain in the complex. We expect the location of clusters of houses of the dead to have influenced not only later burials but also later clusters of dwelling-houses. However, tensions between the builders of these two types of structures and their increasingly contrasting locations may have led to different mortuary treatment for 'locals' and 'outsiders' buried at Alsónyék.

The final aspect of monumentality concerned the sheer cumulative frequency of burials over such a large area of the Alsónyék complex (Fig. 14). Each new person buried there contributed to the fame of the place as well as receiving their share of fame, whether they died from tuberculosis or received a 'normal' or 'deviant' burial (OA/Chapman 2010). It was the exceptional size of the Alsónyék mortuary congregation that created a regional centre.

3.2.4 Performance and Open Area

The availability of formal open spaces in the Lengyel complex seems to have been limited. Performance on the other hand was a frequent experience, involving grave digging, body manipulations (carrying, placing in position, adorning), making sacrifices, food preparations, grave good deposition, chanting, crying, singing or other mourning and celebratory practices. The construction of the unique houses of the dead (Fig. 15) started early in the sequence and continued late. They inevitably concentrated the experience at the time of burial but acted as a constant visual focus of commemorating rituals and ceremonies. The relationship of these houses to the

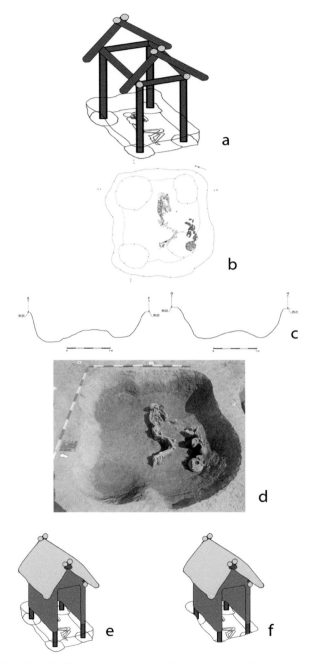

Figure 15 (b)–(d) Plan and section of Grave 10B/6537, Alsónyék (source: Zalai-Gaál et al. 2012, Abb. 8); (a), (e)–(f) reconstruction of its House of the Dead (source: Stuart Johnston)

identity of the deceased and their wider role as a structuring element in the ceremonialism of an ever-expanding burial ground cannot yet be assessed. We do not yet know the complete distribution of houses of the dead by grave group but the dated examples show visually impressive clustering in a few grave groups (e.g., Groups 13 and 56), with single houses in other groups (e.g., Group 14 and 57). However, their restriction to Alsónyék underlines the site's importance by combining the symbolism of both a landmark and a timemark in the formality of the burial rituals. The prominence of large bovids, both wild and domestic (Nyerges & Biller 2015), in the faunal sample emphasises the importance of communal feasting, whether at the grave-side or in domestic practices.

Another important aspect of performance concerns movement. The context of movement at Alsónyék was the sheer size of the complex, requiring twenty to thirty minutes to cross the 1.5 km-long site. Those walking from one end to the other would have passed by over fifty grave groups, many with houses of the dead at their core, as well as many clusters of dwelling houses. Moreover, the arrival of the deceased from other settlements was doubtless accompanied by formal processions at least within the site perimeter, which probably culminated at a ceremony outside a house of the dead. These processions cemented the growing desire of 'outsiders' to be buried at Alsónyék and enhanced burial performance.

3.2.5 Congregational Catchment

In contrast to the Starčevo and Sopot populations, the Lengyel group in general, and the Lengyel persons buried at Alsónyék in particular, were characterised by low mobility (Depaermentier et al. 2020b). This result of strontium isotopic studies (Depaermentier et al. 2020a) is at odds with the proposed nucleation of more than 1,000 people, whether they moved to Alsónyék as living or were brought there as deceased. Mitigation of this discrepancy by future expansion of the pool of individuals sampled for Sr and O isotopes from Alsónyék, together with a wider exploration of the underlying geology to cover a catchment of 30–50 km radius, would benefit the coalescent model more than the mortuary congregation, since people coalesceing at Alsónyék probably came from a wider catchment. The paucity of coeval settlements hampers the investigation of both explanations, with Mórágy, the eponymous site of Lengyel and Várdomb all potentially contributing to the Alsónyék mortuary congregation (OA/Regenye et al. 2020) (Fig. 13). An assumption of the impracticability of transporting dead bodies beyond one day's walk to the mortuary congregation site suggests a 20 km radius for the Alsónyék social catchment. The presence of three dietary outliers in the Lengyel isotopic plot (Bayliss et al. 2016, fig. 9) supports the idea of the burial of migrants at the mortuary centre.

At a wider scale, the concentration of exotic objects in Alsónyék graves points securely to extensive trade and exchange networks. *Dentalium* and *Spondylus* ornaments deriving from the Adriatic or the Aegean, Alpine jadeite axes, light and heavy copper ornaments and Szentgál radiolarite conclusively demonstrate overlapping and complementary exchange networks – a result contrasting with the low mobility of the Lengyel people at Alsónyék. The relatively low fertility of the local soils in the 3 km local catchment at Alsónyék – dominated by meadow soils with some skeletal soils and little brown forest soil – not only limited the local population but also renders improbable the creation of an exchangeable agricultural surplus, although cattle-breeding on the meadow soils could have provided higher surplus potential (Depaermentier et al. 2020a) (here Fig. 13 and Online Appendix I/3 and OA Figs. 3.1–3.6). It is equally likely that the fame of the Alsónyék mortuary congregation elicited the deposition of special, exotic grave goods in the graves of those brought into the centre.

3.3 Conclusions

Rather than a coalescent community of which an excessively high proportion would have required burial, we propose that Alsónyék was primarily a place of mortuary congregation for locals as well as deceased brought from other settlements. This practice began on a small scale, with an enormous expansion c. 4700 cal BC, bringing Alsónyék a regional fame for burial. This striking form of congregation site differed as much from the Trypillia megasite congregations of the living as it did from the megasites of the Central and Western Mediterranean, to which we now turn.

4 Neolithic and Copper Age Sites in Southern Europe

4.1 Introduction

In Section 3, we focussed on German megasites with little evidence for dwelling and a Lengyel megasite dominated by a mortuary domain juxtaposed with intensive dwelling. In this chapter, we move westwards into Southern Europe to examine three regions whose sites show some parallels with the Central European megasites (Table 3). In Southern Italy, ditched enclosures formed the primary settlement form in the Tavoliere plain from the earliest known farming period, with the megasite phenomenon occurring only after several centuries. By contrast, ditched enclosures were rare in the Early Neolithic of Southern France and Southern Iberia, with megasites occurring in later periods character-ised by more settlement aggregation, elaborate material culture, striking mortu-ary remains and the formation of regional polities. The regional chronologies are presented below (Fig. 16).

Table 3 Large Neolithic Settlement Sites and Megasites in the Southern Mediterranean

Name & Region	Date (cal BC)	Maximum Size (ha)	Principal Features	Reference
Tavoliere, Italy				
Passo di Corvo (Fig. 17)	5000–4500	104.5	Double- or triple-ditched main enclosure with c. 120 C-ditches and single-ditched annexe with 9 C-ditches.	Seager Thomas 2020, 223.
Masseria Fragella	6th Millennium	55	Inner and outer ditched enclosures	OA/Jones, G. D. B. 1987.
Posta d'Innanzi	6th Millennium	68	Oval single-ditched inner and double-ditched middle enclosure, with partial outer enclosure.	Seager Thomas 2020, 216–7.
Motta del Lupo	6th Millennium	>60	Multi-ditched sub-oval enclosure with possible annexe to NorthWest.	Seager Thomas 2020, 260–1.
SW France				
St-Michel-du-Touch	4100–2550	20	2 palisades, 26 interrupted ditch segments and 305 cobbled surfaces.	Vaquer 1990.
Villeneuve-Tolosane (Fig. 17)	4200–3800	30	100-m-long palisade, many ditch complexes, well and 350 cobbled surfaces.	Vaquer 1990.

Table 3 (cont.)

Name & Region	Date (cal BC)	Maximum Size (ha)	Principal Features	Reference
Iberia				
Valencina de la Concepción (Fig. 19)	3200–2300	450	See Section 4.5.	García Sanjuán et al. 2018.
Perdigões (Fig. 18)	3500–2000	26	13 concentric ditches, many rock-cut, opposite valley with >100 megalithic tombs.	Valera et al. 2014.
Marroquíes Bajos	2800–1500	113	Inner banked enclosure with 5 concentric ditches.	OA/Castro López et al. 2006.
Alcalar	3rd Millennium	20–40	Enclosure with central group of mounds, with 16 mounds outside.	OA/Moran & Perreira 2009.
Porto Torrão	Late 4th–early 3rd millennia	>100 (? 500)	Double-ditched enclosure with 3 tholoi and hypogea.	OA/Rodriguez 2014.

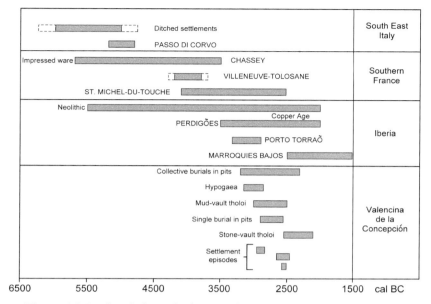

Figure 16 Regional chronologies, Southern Italy, Southern France and Southern Iberia (source: authors, re-drawn by Lauren Woodard)

Manuel Fernández-Götz's characterisation of the Iron Age as: 'the more divisive the society, the more space is divided' (OA/Fernández-Götz & Krause 2016, 15) is relevant here. Space was divided up with visible features such as banks and palisades or less visible cut features such as ditches, often interrupted. Perimeter banks and house walls were rare, while palisades were found on only a few parts of the two large Chasséen enclosures. The vast majority of division was accomplished through digging ditches, which demarcated significant places in the landscapes and structured access to/from interiors. The most important element of a cut feature was the relationship it created with the past – whether earlier cultural features (the ancestral past) or with natural sediments (nature) (OA/Chapman 2000). Digging a pit or a ditch into nature meant establishing an exchange with an undifferentiated past; the taking of ancestral natural materials, with the exchange deferred until later deposition in the cut feature. In the case of Perdigões (Portugal), the performance of excavating one ditch by extracting 14,323m³ of rock was followed by removal of the rock from the circuit rather than the construction of a bank (Valera 2012), leaving a ditch that welcomed many special deposits. The pits inside many of the Iberian enclosure ditches usually contained special deposits, whose elaboration in terms of materials used and sequence of action increased with time.

Such exchanges were central to both large and small sites, even in small unenclosed sites with pit deposition.

There was an important temporal tension between permanence and change at the larger sites. While Valera (OA/2006) has emphasised the permanent state of flux at enclosures, with occupants sharing new experiences as design merged with new building, site duration sometimes exceeded a millennium, with continuity of place related to the ritual or cosmological focus. Moreover, the excavation of many site ditches in segments meant different groups mobilising their own construction labour (OA/Díaz-del-Río 2006). Such constructions were dispersed in time as well as space, with a network of social relations of mutual support based upon feasts, gatherings and projects. It is thus not surprising that, the longer the site use, the more probable the polyfocal nature of performance.

In his discussion of Iberian enclosures, Marquez (OA/2003) denies the general separation of sacred and profane. However, the dialectic of this relationship varied through time and place: indeed, the relationship between dwelling and burial became problematic. In the Copper Age at Perdigões, the boundary between the living ('domestic' discard) and the dead (bodily discard or burial) became blurred over time through the diversification of mortuary practices, which increasingly became the site's key performances. It is intriguing that communities used the commingling of sacred and profane to transcend *their own* spatial divisions *sensu* Fernández-Götz! Thus we can re-evaluate in two ways Hurtado's (2006) striking claim that enclosures acted as a monumentalisation of domestic space. The first is that the profane must be included in many aspects of this vertical up-scaling process. The second is that ditches – even 6 m deep ditches – could have been visible 'monuments' only on a local scale of 10s–100s of metres. There is an evident tension between social memory and visibility in ditched enclosures, which was worked out locally in diverse ways. We now turn to the three regional sequences.

4.2 Southern Italy

There is a long tradition of enclosing small spaces of up to 4 ha from the start of the Neolithic settlement on the Tavoliere, which cumulatively formed one of the densest site concentrations in Neolithic Europe (OA/Jones, G. D. B. 1987; OA/Hamilton & Whitehouse 2020). These ditched enclosures were often multi-period sites, with up to eight concentric ditches. Only at a later stage, communities started to excavate long, if irregular, stretches of single ditches to enclose what have been called 'Annexes' but which were actually the key part of the new extended sites. In fact, only a handful of large sites, and even fewer small sites (<4 ha), consisted of both outer and inner (settlement) enclosures.

The largest of these is the megasite of Passo di Corvo, whose main enclosure of 38.5 ha and outer enclosure (annexe) of 64 ha produced a total size of 104.5 ha (Seager Thomas 2020) (here Fig. 17). G. D. B. Jones (OA/1987, 101) described Passo di Corvo as 'the major prehistoric settlement of the Tavoliere'. The key difference between the outer and inner enclosures is the density of smaller C-shaped ditches in the latter, accompanied with intensive deposition, with a relative paucity of C-shaped ditches or finds in the former. The outer enclosures were largely empty spaces – effectively equivalent to the central open spaces in Trypillia sites (see Section 2). Previous authors have proposed defence, stock enclosures and fields for the outer enclosure. We propose, instead, that their primary function was for seasonal congregation for people from the local and other communities. The Passo di Corvo outer enclosure would have attracted visitors from a social catchment of the entire Tavoliere, estimated at 5,000 people (OA/Robb 2007), replacing the earlier, localised network of clustered interactions between a few closely-spaced enclosures (OA/Whitehouse 2013). The digging of the outer ditch defined not only the meeting space but also membership of a regional community, such as a lineage or clan. The years of seasonal labour (OA/Brown 1991) did not merely represent the community itself in action – it *was* the community in action. We suggest that the guardians of the outer enclosure lived in the C-shaped enclosures on the top of the site's hill.

It is important to note that ceremonial events were not restricted to the congregation space at Passo di Corvo. There were many small-scale ceremonial acts and ritual performances – if few staged mortuary events – in the open areas in the inner enclosure, including feasting and special deposition of objects and body parts (for details, see OA/Tinè 1983; OA/Skeates 2000). The congregation area hosted the larger events, including 'beating of the bounds' (for explanation, see Section 1.3.2), regular deposition in the outer ditch and other less materially rich events (music, dancing, storytelling). While the excavation data show that similar practices occurred in the inner and outer enclosures at Passo di Corvo, the scale of the congregation and the intensity of the meetings between hundreds or even thousands of participants is what differentiated this site from all others on the Tavoliere.

4.3 Southern France

The later Neolithic in Southern France, designated as the Chassey group (Vaquer 1990), comprised a wide range of small settlement sites, with sizes between 0.07 ha and 5 ha, as well as enclosed sites attesting to both dwelling and display practices (OA/Phillips 1982). There were no sites as large as Passo di Corvo in Italy but two sites in the Middle Garonne Basin – St-Michel-du-Touche and Villeneuve-Tolosane – stand out relationally as the largest sites in

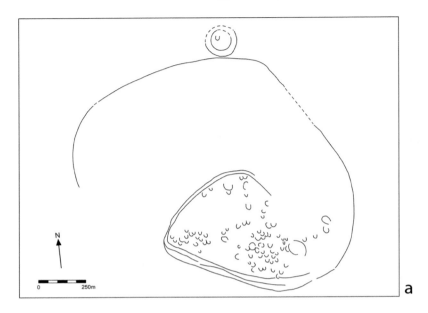

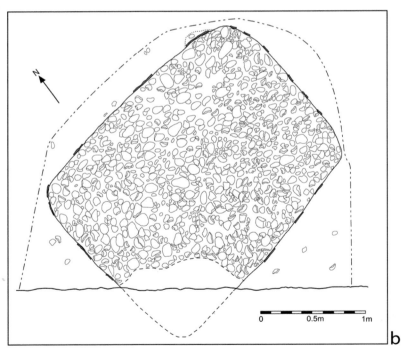

Figure 17 (a) Plan of Passo di Corvo (Whitehouse 2013, fig. 2.1G, amended by Lauren Woodard); (b) Plan of cobbled feature 215, Villeneuve-Tolosane (source: Simonnet 1980, fig. 2.2a, amended by Lauren Woodard)

the region – the latter over 400 times bigger than the smallest open site. Both sites show multi-period enclosure features, including ditches and palisades. Each successive extension of the enclosed area provided open areas for meetings. Cobbled surfaces (Fig. 17) sunk in pits provided the most frequent features at both sites and at other, smaller sites. We propose that these features were cooking pits where heated cobbles roasted entire skeletons, most often of cattle. A meat rather than a dairy profile of the Villeneuve cattle is consistent with feasting and the Garonne sites had less varied diets than those nearer the coast in Languedoc (OA/Herrscher & Le Bras-Goude 2010). Strontium isotopic mobility studies have shown that Languedoc residents were buried in the Garonne sites and vice versa (OA/Goude et al. 2012). The range of evidence is consistent with congregation sites at St. Michel and Villeneuve but without the regional focus of Passo di Corvo in the Tavoliere.

4.4 South-West Iberia

The use of aerial photography and geophysics has rarely had such a dramatic effect on a region's archaeology as in South-West Iberia, with a new class of ditched enclosures of central importance since the 1990s. Although 60 per cent of these sites covered <1 ha (Valera 2012), Late Neolithic enclosures grew to 10 ha, with a further, Copper Age expansion to 110 ha. As with the apparently unenclosed megasite of Valencina de la Concepción (for extended discussion, see Section 4.5), excavations have demonstrated the multi-period, polyfocal nature of these major complexes. While a small Neolithic settlement preceded the Alcalar enclosure, cromlechs constituted the earliest monuments at both Perdigões and Porto Torrão. Multiple concentric ditches typified Perdigões (13 ditches: Fig. 18) and Monte da Contenda (17–19 ditches).

The rarity of banks and houses at most ditched enclosures and the high frequency of cut pit features meant that the most monumental features were often tombs, especially in the Copper Age. This spatial expansion of the mortuary domain was integrated with the burial of larger numbers of bodies/body parts with a higher proportion of exotic grave goods to create a new type of person-place, often interpreted as high-status. Sitting in a monumental landscape, the Perdigões enclosures were unique in having entrances constructed to face east to a valley containing over 100 megalithic tombs (Valera 2012).

There is an ongoing debate over the level of permanent settlement in ditched enclosures – if any dwelling at all to intensive occupation (Hurtado 2006). Given the importance of querns for food production, there is a striking similarity in their density at open sites, ditched enclosures and fortified sites (OA/Risch 2013). The focus of open areas for congregation at complexes with multiple ditches became

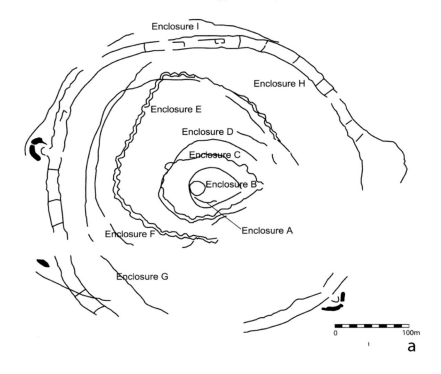

a

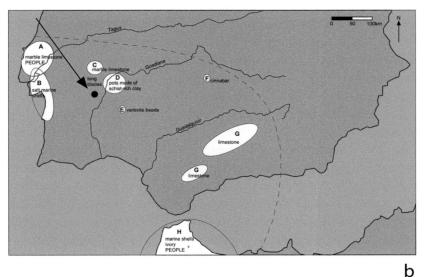

b

Figure 18 (a) Plan of Perdigões (source: Valera 2012, fig. 2.3/1, re-drawn by
Lauren Woodard); (b) exotic exchange and non-local people buried at Perdigões:
Areas: A – Estremadura (marble, limestone, people); B – Tagus and Sado
estuaries and coastal Alentejo (marine shells); C – Estremoz – Borba – Vila
Viçosa (marble, limestone); D – Tierra de Barros (pots made of schist-rich clay);

greater, moving ever outwards with time. Larger-scale congregations could have been held in the outer enclosures at Marroquíes Bajos and Porto Torrão.

The congregational catchment of ditched enclosure communities can be studied through investigations of both human bones and objects. In the Middle Neolithic, a complex mortuary network distributed human bones across the landscape from a series of different cemeteries, all of which sent bones to the upland Bom Santo cave (OA/Carvalho et al. 2019). By the Copper Age at Perdigões, most of the large sample of sixty-nine individuals so far analysed for strontium isotopes came from outside the local area, with several persons matching signals from the Lisbon Peninsula, in contrast to the local origins of persons buried in dolmens (OA/Valera et al. 2020) (Fig. 18). Dental analysis shows North African influences in the distribution of some non-metric traits – possibly the result of genetic exchanges with North African groups (OA/Cunha 2015). This result is supported by the deposition of African elephant ivory in tholos tombs, often with Sicilian amber. The regular acquisition of stone and metals for Perdigões (Fig. 18) and Alcalar from sources up to 70 km away indicates that this was their likely congregational catchment zone.

4.5 Valencina de la Concepción

Of all the sites discussed in this Element, Valencina is the only one for which the core premise of congregation has been mooted (García Sanjuán et al. 2018, 280; Martínez-Sevilla et al. 2020). The coastal site was located on the flat, fertile Aljarafe plateau, at 150 masl, overlooking the Guadalquivir valley and a coeval marine inlet. The AMS dates for Valencina show a long occupation from 3200 to 2300 cal BC (García Sanjuán et al. 2018), covering most of the Iberian Copper Age. It is also one of the largest complexes, at c. 450 ha, and one of the most intensively investigated sites in Spain, with nearly 130 excavation campaigns, starting in the 19th century (Costa Caramé et al. 2010) (Fig. 19). The most prominent archaeological features in the present landscape are the impressive tholoi of La Pastora (Fig. 21) and Matarrubilla that once were part of a wider megalithic landscape that included mud-vaulted tholoi, the most

---

Caption for Figure 18 (cont.)

E – Pico Centeno (variscite); F – Almaden (cinnabar); G – Jurassic silicified limestone outcrops, Betic Mountains; H – western North Africa (marine shells, ivory, people). As yet unsourced raw materials include gold, amber and rock crystal (source: OA/Valera 2017, fig. 3.1, re-drawn by Lauren Woodard)

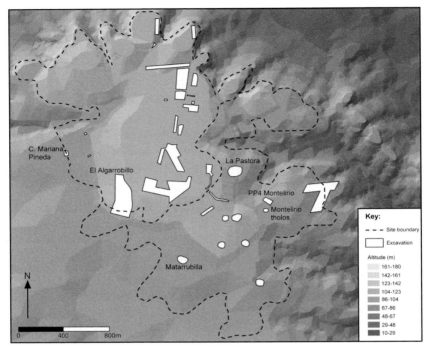

Figure 19 Site plan of Valencina de la Concepción, showing excavated areas (source: Costa Caramé et al. 2010, fig. 2.2, with additions by Lauren Woodard)

impressive of which was Montelirio (OA/Fernández Flores et al. 2016). These funerary features were complemented by artificial caves (*hypogaea*) and pits with collective or individual burials, with both complete and partial bodies being common throughout the site. Last but not least are the numerous negative features, some of which showed clear evidence for production of metal and ivory, while others were more readily associated with domestic discard (Costa Caramé et al. 2010). The sheer number of investigations conducted by almost as many different teams has led not only to great disparity in the level of system-atisation and recording of the archaeological evidence but also to contrasting views about the nature of the site. For instance, Nocete Calvo et al. (OA/2008) have argued for Valencina as a state-level metallurgical centre – a view opposed by García Sanjuán and Murillo-Barroso (OA/2013). This lack of an integrated approach has plagued the understanding of Valencina for a long time; only in the last decade have huge strides been made to overcome the piecemeal utilisation of the available archaeological data, in which compelling interpretations of certain sectors/sites (e.g. García Sanjuán et al. 2019) match holistic attempts at the understanding of the site (García Sanjuán et al. 2018, Martínez-Sevilla et al. 2020). In Online Appendix II, we offer an assessment of the implications of the current views about Valencina, as well as a breakdown of the occupation in time and space into five phases in order to overcome definitional issues with dwelling and burial.

As with the other megasites we discuss, the question of why Valencina was so large has hardly been directly addressed. We propose that Valencina was a congregation site and its size was a consequence of both increasing place-value and internal development. The accumulation of cultural memory and place-based associations over nine centuries of occupation created a unique reputation for Valencina but not one without tensions. The multiplicity of domestic and mortuary foci suggests great dynamism and inter-focus contrasts in site development, leading to spatial displacement rather than 'local' transcendence of differences – all of which required a larger site area. Moreover, Valencina is a summary statement of the Iberian Copper Age settlement pattern containing dispersed dwelling and production areas, monumental tomb architecture, ditched enclosures and non-megalithic burials, only lacking the walled enclosures so typical of 3rd millennium Iberia. The incredible artefactual wealth of the site is not simply a result of long-term accumulation and random deposition but a further summary statement of key resources and the materialisation of wide exchange networks. Thus, the importance of *dehesa* forest management and land use in 3rd millennium Spain led to the crafting at Valencina of miniature images of pigs and acorns from ivory, while the prestigious rearing of equids (OA/Harrison, R. J. 1985) stimulated their fired clay representations and wide-ranging personal networks produced many exotic deposits. These are just a few aspects of a much wider and very diverse pattern that due to lack of space we cannot elaborate on here.

4.5.1 Scale

The size of Valencina, at 450 ha, has implications for the huge scale of social practices in an area not closely defined by a perimeter earthwork. The scale of occupation is indicated by the estimated number of 40,000 prehistoric features, based on extrapolation from the PP4-Montelirio sector excavations (Fig. 20). An as yet undefined proportion of these features can be related to congregational practices, of which a classic example is the compelling evidence for feasting in Structure 10.024 (García Sanjuán 2017). The unprecedented intensity of occupation should be integrated with the scale of consumption of certain artefacts and also the proliferation of special kinds of deposition. Currently there are several types of artefacts and materials in Valencina that are either most numerous or unique in comparison with other sites (Fig. 21). Not only is

Figure 20 Detail of excavation plan of the La Pastora – Montelirio sector (source: García Sanjuán et al. 2018, fig. 3.6: re-drawn by Lauren Woodard)

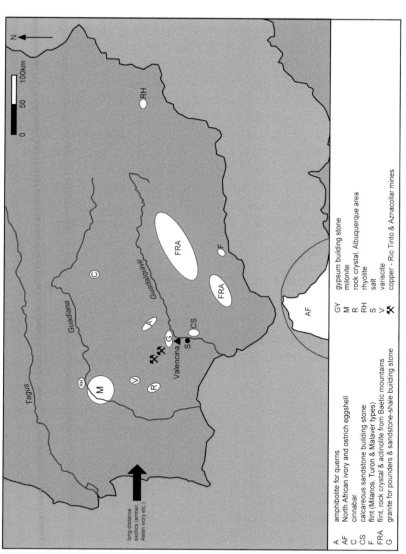

Figure 21 Exotic exchange at Valencina de la Concepción: A – amphibolite for querns; AF – North African ivory and ostrich eggshell; C – cinnabar; CS – calcareous sandstone building stone; F – flint (Milanos, Turón & Malaver types); FRA – flint, rock-crystal and actinolite from Baetic Mountains; G – granite for pounders and sandstone-shale building stone; GY – gypsum building stone; M – milonite; R – rock crystal, Albuquerque area; RH – rhyolite; S – salt; V – variscite; mining symbol – Río Tinto and Aznacóllar copper mines; (source: authors, re-drawn by Lauren Woodard)

Valencina the sole site so far with both Asian and African ivory but also the quantity of ivory, at 8.8 kg, with 7.9 kg found in just two features (Montelirio tholos and PP4-Montelirio) far exceeded the amount at other sites (e.g. 1.7 kg at Perdigões). Local production of exquisitely crafted unique objects is attested and the site has provided the greatest number of gold (OA/Murillo-Barroso et al. 2015) and rock-crystal (OA/Morgado Rodriguez et al. 2016) artefacts of any Iberian Copper Age complex. The quantity of Sicilian amber far exceeded the usual low-level consumption, with only one site – Anta Grande do Zambujeiro – showing a comparable quantity of this exotic material (OA/Odriozola et al. 2019). These exotics attest not only to a special scale of consumption but also a huge reach in the scale of networking.

It is through the totality of the evidence and the cumulative value of interactions that the uniqueness of Valencina's scale of practices can be judged. It is in the concentration, combination and re-combination of varied practices – including the number of burials (probably exceeding 1,000 individuals), variety and quantity of exotics, variety of monument types and examples of unique craftsmanship – that makes the scale of Valencina stand out in Copper Age Iberia.

4.5.2 Temporality (Fig. 22 and Online Appendix II)

The groundbreaking cooperation that led to a comprehensive dating programme (García Sanjuán et al. 2018) underlines the cumulative duration of social practices at Valencina, matched at few other Iberian sites (Table 3). There was a strong contrast between the seeming permanence of the mortuary tholoi and the episodic utilisation of domestic areas, some even lacking clear residential traces. But the frequency of return visits to Valencina contributed to the narrative of an ever-changing regional population with material and emotional links to their congregation centre, turning the latter into a place more permanent than many small settlements.

Paradoxically, the precision of AMS dates for each site hinders a straightforward comparison of diachronic change, which is more readily achieved using 200-year time-slices (Fig. 22) (Online Appendix II). There is an inevitability about the dynamic, changing use of different parts of the site through the long occupation, with life starting with burial practices in at least two zones, finishing with an ancestral megalithic landscape with continued burial and sandwiching episodes of burial, production, permanent residence and seasonal visits of various durations. The upstanding tholos La Pastora (Fig. 23) encapsulated temporal relations linking the past (the inclusion in the roof of an altered capstone from another megalith), the present (ongoing mortuary usage) and the future (a spectacular but undated hoard of

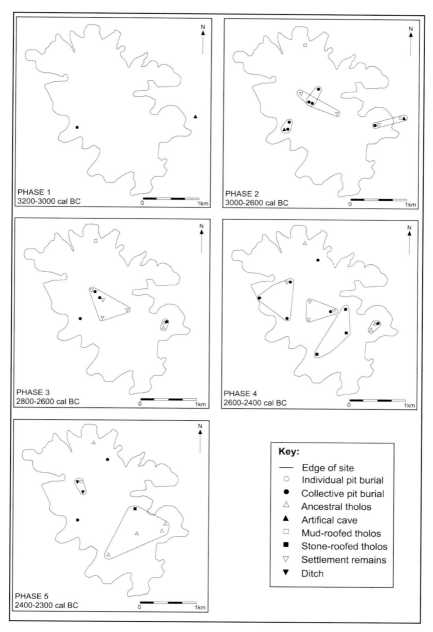

Figure 22 Plans of the five phases of Valencina de la Concepción
(source: authors, re-drawn by Lauren Woodard)

a

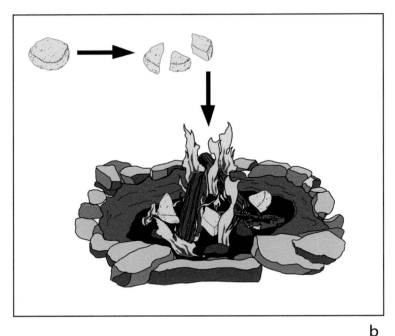

b

Figure 23 (a) photo of La Pastora tholos (source: authors); (b) reconstruction
of the grindstone-breaking and burning ritual (source: Lauren Woodard)

twenty-nine spearheads near the tholos (García Sanjuán 2017). The selection of
different spatial foci for mortuary practices contrasted with the continuity of use of
the central settlement area, with the different 'local' identities implicit in spatially

disparate foci perhaps the main reason for the lack of an all-embracing perimeter enclosure.

Valencina must very often have stood out among its contemporary counterparts with its unique use of space, which in its congregational function accommodated both continuity (settlement foci) and change (from collective to individual burial). Some thirty to forty generations of people would have built up a unique combination of architectural foci and cumulative social memory through repeated acts of production and deposition.

4.5.3 Monumentality

An elemental contrast central to understanding Valencina is the difference between earthen and stone monuments (OA/Pauketat et al. 2015). The former included hypogaea, pit burials, ditches and settlement features, all except the massive ditches requiring modest labour, and suffered from gradually diminishing visibility after use. The latter were tholoi that transcended generational change through their visibility and permanence and required substantial labour, not least the transport of many heavy blocks from their sources 15–30 km distant. In the absence of what would have been a monumental perimeter earthwork, the principal monuments were these tholoi, whose stone cores maintained their structural stability despite loss of barrow height. The colour and textural differences between the three main geologies used at La Pastora (Fig. 23) and Matarrubilla – sandstone-shale, calcareous sandstone and granite, as well as the exotic gypsum (OA/Caceres et al. 2019) – heightened the magnificence of the constructions, which were emphasised even further by the exposure of natural, marine-related 'motifs' in the sandstones. The deviation of La Pastora and Matarrubilla from the regional orientational norms added an astronomical significance to the tombs underlining their monumentality, which would have gained in prominence in social memory over the centuries. The choreography of the burials at Montelirio suggests this monument was a 'sanctuary' more than simply a tomb.

4.5.4 Open Area

There is a tension between the presence of a small ditched enclosure in the interior and the absence of a perimeter ditch, leaving undefined a huge unenclosed site and vast empty areas. In comparison with the planned interior of Trypillia megasites (Section 2), the apparent lack of planning at Valencina may give the impression that the empty areas are the random by-products of the arrangements of pits, huts, ditches, graves and megaliths – lacking formalisation and therefore meaning. However, it is the inter-connections between sectors that shows that nothing about Valencina was random, not least the staged deposition of grinding stones across the whole site (Martínez-Sevilla et al. 2020) or the burial of individuals with special diets (with high ^{8}N15 values) in megaliths and those with 'normal' diets in non-megalithic foci (OA/Díaz-Zorita Bonilla 2017). This organic growth left enough empty space for congregation, ceremonies, markets, negotiations over elite leadership and dispute resolution, as well as perhaps more competitive practices in terms of mortuary prominence (Fig. 19). The cohesive component of congregation was shown by inter-linked domestic deposition, while competition between visiting groups was underscored by mortuary differences.

The proposal is that this spatial arrangement was an interplay of all those components characterising the Iberian Copper Age (small open area settlements, ditched enclosures, megalithic monuments), which more often than not are discussed separately, and which came together at Valencina in a unique way. Although the visual attraction of the tholoi should not be underestimated, no single site type took precedence because of the linkages between enchained social relations and repeated acts of deposition. Instead, there was a tension between existing foci, with spatial displacement of small groups showing rupture, tension and forgetting in contrast to the continuity of place-use and memory, which showed consensus and acceptance of the status quo. The replacement of entire mortuary types by others (e.g., *hypogaea* replaced by tholoi) shows a more fundamental change – development through contrast with preceding practices and forms.

4.5.5 Performance

There was enormous potential for performative actions at Valencina. Restrictions of space limit our discussion to only three examples – two related to mortuary practices and the third to non-funerary deposition.

Collective burial in pits spanned the entire sequence at Valencina, with specific pits often receiving burials over several centuries (e.g. Structure 1 in El Algarrobillo) and offering a window to the underworld and the ancestors. The benefits of allowing the participation of a large group of mourners in the accompanying choreographed rituals and displays was counter-balanced by the continued inconvenience of repeated excavation of the upper levels of the pit fill, which, however, allowed the frequent and deliberate disturbance of ancestral deposits. But, despite the monumental alternative, this mode of burial was accepted for centuries.

In contrast, the same journey to the underworld in the tholoi was choreographed in more discrete stages, which were partly restricted to ritual specialists. Only during the open funeral procession could the larger group of mourners see the colours and contrasts of cinnabar and the beads on the mortuary costumes used to adorn the Montelirio burials or the glistening brightness of the rock-crystal. Those witnesses remaining outside the tomb would probably have experienced poignant moments for social memories. The later stages of the funeral were framed and visually restricted by the monumental passage to the chamber. There was also a fundamentally different phenomenological experience for those chosen few participants for going to the underworld and back – the partial visibility of the natural 'art' motifs in the flickering darkness (OA/Cáceres et al. 2019) and the triggering of other sensory experiences by the smell of decaying bodies and the accompanying nausea.

The exemplary study of Valencina grindstones demonstrated a high percentage of fragmentation and burning of these heavy objects (Martínez-Sevilla et al. 2020). Regardless of whether the two processes were inter-related, each would have created its own spectacle. Smashing an object intimately related to food production would have been a dramatic event, with skilled practitioners producing special sound effects. The flames of the burning ceremonies marked the end of the pits through a ritual killing, with flames appearing to come out of the pits and ditches (Fig. 23).

4.5.6 Congregation Catchment

There is no doubt that people, animals and things were coming to the Valencina congregation from near and far. One-third of the 33 individuals in the strontium isotopic analysis were identified as non-local (OA/Díaz-Zorita Bonilla 2017), although their origins were not specified. A further set of 65 individuals was subjected to FRUITS dietary reconstruction, with one very clear outlier consuming far more marine and freshwater fish than the remainder, with their pattern of a C3-plant-based diet with differentiated intake of terrestrial protein (García Sanjuán et al. 2018). Given that once Valencina was in effect a coastal site, one possibility to be checked in the future is that the high-consuming-fish individual was local, while the rest of the sampled individuals came from further afield. The bovid with a non-local oxygen isotopic signature shows visitors to the congregation bringing their own animals for feasting (OA/Díaz-Zorita Bonilla et al. 2017), while current evidence for the Schlepp effect of off-site animal butchery suggest the transport of the meatiest joints for consumption and deposition at PP-Matarrubilla and Calle Mariana Pineda s/n (García Sanjuán 2017).

The objects deposited at Valencina may be divided into local, exotic and mega-exotic (Fig. 21), with some objects of ivory and copper produced on-site and others such as flint brought to Valencina as finished objects. The origins of grindstones and the transport of heavy rocks (up to 1 ton) for tholos-construction defined the local catchment of 30 km, while the procession carrying the gypsum monolith to

Matarrubilla showed visitors coming from 50 km distance. All the other materials demonstrate participation in wide-ranging exchange networks with other Iberian and North African communities. Exotic materials included flint from the Baetic Mountains of the Malaga–Granada regions, a flint dagger from an as yet unidenti-fied source outside Southern Iberia, cinnabar from the Almadén region of central Spain and variscite from Zamora, north-west Spain, while two possible sources for rock-crystal were the Baetic Mountains and the schist–greywacke zone of the Iberian Massif in central Spain. The mega-exotics include North African ivory and ostrich eggshell, Sicilian amber and Levantine Asian ivory. The copper spearheads in the latest deposit, near La Pastora, were probably inspired by Levantine metallurgy (García Sanjuán 2017). In comparison with the Perdigões exotic objects (Fig. 18) and in line with its greater social significance as a massive congregation centre, the Valencina exchange network showed a greater diversity of materials procured from a far wider range of sources.

4.6 Conclusions

The repeated occupation, deposition and burial at Valencina de la Concepción created a patchwork of rich cultural memories, which, by the latest deposition, stretched back almost a millennium. This summary of site and monument forms that typified the Iberian Copper Age made Valencina a unique congregation place to which thousands of visitors returned repeatedly, bringing some of the rarest as well as the most common objects of the age for deposition in special and quotidian places. The scale of performances and celebrations of the annual meeting made Valencina one of the most famous sites in Western Europe, with its reputation spreading out to many regions and thousands of sites.

5 Bronze Age Megasites
5.1 Introduction

Few European prehistorians would dispute that Bronze Age networks con-nected more people over longer distances with more objects – especially metal – than in previous times. However, there is far less agreement over the political and military consequences of these changes (OA/Kienlin 2020; Hansen & Krause 2018). A focal point of development came in the Late Bronze Age, starting c. 1400 cal BC, with the construction of over 1,000 hillforts from Central Germany to the Carpathian Basin (Hansen & Krause 2018) accompanying major innovations in weaponry and armour. Fortifications create a major challenge to what Keeley (OA/1996) has called 'a pacified prehistory' and challenge us to explain what was one of the greatest transform-ations of the Bronze Age.

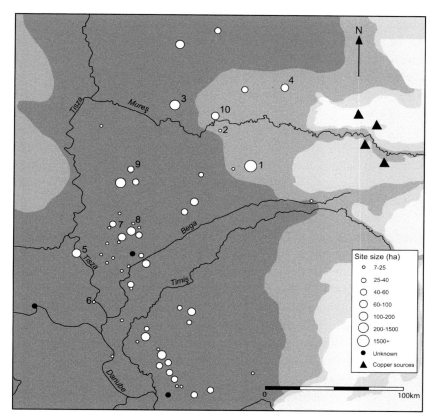

Figure 24 Map of Late Bronze Age sites in South-Eastern part of the Middle Danube Basin, with copper sources (sources: Molloy et al. 2020, fig. 1.1; OA/ Mareş 2002, Harta 1: re-drawn by Lauren Woodard)

For Keeley et al. (2007, 79), 'the symbolism of fortifications was always predicated on their military functions'. Although not all enclosing features (or '*enceintes*') were defensive in nature, enclosures *could* still be defensive even if they lacked the three key traits of a fortification – V-sectioned ditches, complex gateways and bastions (Keeley et al. 2007). Defences protected a wide range of the elements of everyday life, whether resources and possessions, homes and special places such as shrines, as well as transcending their military functions to increase status and monumental performance.

Located in the South-Eastern part of the Middle Danube Basin (Fig. 24), the lowland region of the Banat reveals the greatest concentration of large enclosed/ fortified sites, termed 'megaforts' (Molloy et al. 2020, 293), in Bronze Age Europe, with the highest number of LBA gold finds in the Basin (OA/Mozsolics 1973) found in the key zone of the Lower Mureş/Maros valley. In the preceding

Middle Bronze Age, the principal form of central place was the tell, whose elevated occupation levels were often defended with encircling ditches rather than banks (Gogâltan 2017). The main tell in the region has been identified as Pecica, which, at its peak, was linked to the distribution of horses and metal-work throughout the Carpathian Basin (OA/Nicodemus & O'Shea 2019) (Fig. 24/Site 10). Although tells founded in the MBII or III phases are not known in the Lower Mureş, the MBA Phase I tells formed antecedent monuments still visible in the landscape, playing significant roles in several LBA megaforts (Table 4). The lack of chronological overlap between MBA fortified tells and LBA megaforts does not preclude a shared *habitus* of living in a clearly delineated, highly structured enclosed space.

Molloy et al. (2020, fig. 1.1 & table 1.1) have identified a site hierarchy based on scale and size, design and distribution, with seven size-based ranks. Even if the ranking is over-elaborate, it is clear that each megafort in the top rank organised a network of smaller enclosed forts and even smaller unenclosed settlements (Fig. 24/Sites 6–8). Molloy et al. interpret this settlement pattern as a series of multi-local societies under a common political framework, with the construction and maintenance of megaforts a performative form of power. 'Enclosures are a physical embodiment of a recognisable regime that resourced large-scale political ideologies manifested through similar settlement features . . . in a densely settled landscape' (Molloy et al. 2020, 299). But LBA communities structured not only their own fortified settlements. The presence of a linear ditch system almost 10 km in length linking four LBA forts between Variaş and Satchinez shows the landscape scale of land division and territorial control (OA/Dorogostaisky & Hegyi 2017, who cite several other cognate systems) (here, Fig. 25). It was not only at the site level of change from tells to megaforts that LBA social transformations were played out but at the wider landscape scale as well.

5.2 Important Megaforts

The exceptional size of Corneşti-Iarcuri singles the complex out for special discussion (see Section 5.3). Four other well-investigated sites provide a representative selection of the fortified examples of the seventy currently known LBA sites in the Banat (Molloy et al. 2020, fig. 1.1) (here, Fig. 24) – Csanadpalota (400 ha), Idjoš-Gradište (200 ha), Sântana (180 ha) and Munar (15 ha) (for details, see Table 4). All of these sites, which are dated to 1400–900 cal BC, shared a common reliance on both natural and cultural antecedent landscape features (OA/Zvelebil & Beneš 1997). Streams flowed across the enclosed areas, actively influencing the layout of the defensive system, as at Sântana (Fig. 25). The provision of fresh water for animals and humans may

Table 4 Features of selected Late Bronze Age enclosed/fortified complexes, Banat

Site (reference)	Enclosure	Size (total area) (ha)	Antecedent Features	Rampart Length (m)	Estim. Volume of Earth (m³)	Estim. Volume of Timber (m³)	Interior Features	Special Deposition
Corneşti (Heeb et al. 2018) (Figs. 24/site 1 & 26)	I	72	Stream network	3,140	72,000	9,863	Few anomalies	
	II	212	ECA & MBA ring-ditches	5,950	144,000	5,027	Rectangular houses & pits	Burials in II rampart
	III	507		8,230	108,700	6,947*	Few anomalies	
	IV	17 654		15,735	205,785	15,377	Few anomalies	
Sântana (OA/ Gogaltan & Sava 2020) (Figs. 24/ site 4 & 26)	I	14	Stream network; MBA tell nearby	1,524			House cluster	
	II	50		2,860			Few anomalies	
	III	(180)	Rampart built over stream; Baden pits	3,630	237,220		Few anomalies	Burnt daub in ditch
Idjoš-Gradište (Molloy et al. 2020) (Figs. 24/ site 9 & 26)	Citadel	2.5	LN tell; nearby flat cemetery; 40 barrows (?date)					

Table 4 (cont.)

Site (reference)	Enclosure	Size (total area) (ha)	Antecedent Features	Rampart Length (m)	Estim. Volume of Earth (m³)	Estim. Volume of Timber (m³)	Interior Features	Special Deposition
	I	18					Rare buildings; many pits	Sandstone block & skull in ditch
	II	35	Stream cuts enclosure					
	III	130						
	IV	(200)						
Munar (OA/Sava & Gogâltan 2017) (Fig. 24/site 2)	I	0.28						
	II	0.66						
	III	1	Baden sherds, MBA tell				Most anomalies	
	IV	8						
	V	(15)						
Csanadpalota (Szeverényi et al. 2015) (Fig. 24/site 3)		(400)		2.5 linear (4 km)			Ditches and pits	Feasting debris in pits; GS fragments

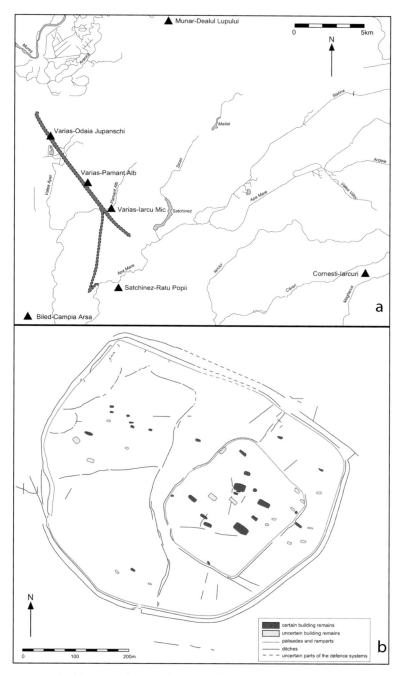

Figure 25 (a) Plan of the Variaş–Satchinez linear ditch system (source: Dorogostaisky & Hegyi 2017, fig. 2.3, re-drawn by Lauren Woodard); (b) Interpretation of geophysical plot, Sântana (source: Gogâltan & Sava 2010, fig. 2.6, re-drawn by Lauren Woodard)

ultimately have been compromised by waste disposal. In three cases, the forts were built next to, or even included, earlier tells – a Late Neolithic tell at Idjoš and MBA tells in the Munar complex and near Sântana. Four barrows were included in the last-named's enclosure, with other barrows outside, while a network of forty barrows forming three linear groupings along palaeo-channels probably pre-dated the Idjoš enclosures (Fig. 26), as did a flat inhum-ation cemetery 1 km distant. These ancestral links to nature and earlier settlers tied the identities of the fort-builders into their local landscapes, legitimising their presence at key nodes in the settlement network.

An important characteristic of these sites is the marked variability in enclosure design. The most importance difference distinguishes the majority of sites, with their concentric *enceintes* (e.g., Sântana: Fig. 25), from the Idjoš example of agglutinative design, where four separate enclosures have been constructed next to one another near the small mound termed the 'citadel' (OA/Marić et al. 2016) (Fig. 26). These designs suggest contrasts not only in temporality, with the obvious sequence of the concentric *enceintes* and the far less clear sequence of the Idjoš enclosures, but also in social relations – building on traditional, ancestral structures in the former, with the possibility of contrasting identities in each enclosure with the latter. The diversity of combination of the same four basic elements – banks (with or without casemate construction), ditches (of varying form), berms and palisades – varied from site to site and sometimes within sites (e.g., the different forms of bank construction in the three banks at Sântana). Special features also occurred, such as the 2.5 km long linear ditch in the centre of the huge Csanadpalota enclosure – reminiscent of the Variaş–Satchinez linear ditch system – or the formalised entrance to the Idjoš citadel, access to which required crossing six ditches. The form of the ditches meant that defence was prioritised at some sites (e.g., the V-sectioned ditch at Sântana Enclosure III) but not at others (V-sectioned ditches were not encountered at Csanadpalota). At Idjoš, the form of ditch 2A, dug in front of an entrance, changed from V-sectioned, so defensive, to a U-shaped profile and finally a shallow, flat-bottomed form (Molloy et al. 2020).

The widespread, indeed essential, use of geophysical investigation at these large sites has also produced widely varying results. Molloy et al.'s (2020) reply to the question of why there were so few house-shaped anomalies at Idjoš was that the architectural design itself left few traces, but this is contradicted at Sântana Enclosure I, with its cluster of impressive rectangular houses in one 60 m x 40 m complex. A series of ditches in Enclosure II at the same site has been interpreted as a delineation of residential areas. This would suggest that the absence of building-type geophysical anomalies may indeed indicate evidence of absence and not the converse. Little evidence for craft production has yet been found at these sites, although slingshot production may have been a local

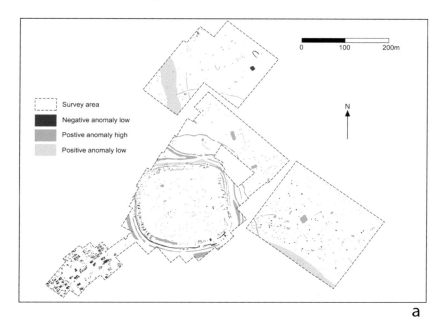

a

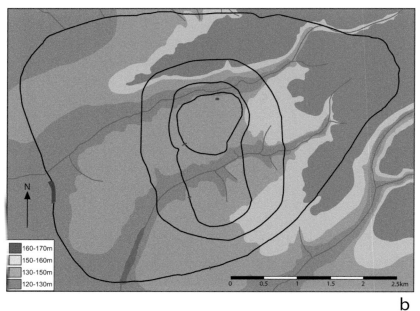

b

Figure 26 (a) Interpretative plan of the geophysical plots, Idjoš –
Gradište complex (source: Molloy et al. 2020, fig. 2.3B, re-drawn by Lauren
Woodard); (b) general plan of Cornești–Iarcuri: red areas – excavated (OA/
Szentmiklosi et al. 2016, fig. 1.1, re-drawn by Lauren Woodard)

skill highly developed at Sântana for resistance to the putative siege postulated at this site. Rather than military preparedness, place-marks in ditches and pits are indicative of special deposition at all of these sites, as in the long life-cycle of certain pits at Idjoš and the deposition of the bones of game animals, perhaps from elite hunting.

Feasting has been claimed at Csanadpalota, where a group of five pits shows evidence for the deposition of feasting remains (e.g., Pit 474, with the bones indicating the consumption of meat weighing 600 kg). The overall faunal sample shows a mix of low-, medium- and high-quality meat cuts for all domestic species and red deer, suggesting both feasting and 'normal' domestic consumption may have relied on all meat qualities (Kassabaum 2019). Large-scale megasite feasting may well have led to different middening practices, with pit middens exhibiting a slower, gradual build-up of feasting remains but still within the year, while open-air middens would have received feasting debris more rapidly. This feasting and other evidence suggested to Szeverényi et al. (2015, 101) the interpretation of Csanadpalota as 'a fortified ritual centre where a large community gathered from time to time to carry out various rituals' – a rather more positive conclusion than Molloy et al's (2020, 310): 'we would struggle to rule (Idjoš) out as a venue for gatherings or events'.

There can be little doubt of the necessity of large numbers of people for the construction of massive dump ramparts at these sites. Estimates for the 3.63 km long Sântana Enclosure III rampart (Fig. 25) suggest a requirement of over $237,000m^3$ of earth, mostly sourced from the excavation of the adjoining ditch (Gogâltan & Sava 2010). Calculations using the same methods as discussed for Cornești (Section 5.3.3 and Online Appendix III) but using the smallest estimated workforce show the requirement of between four and twenty construction seasons for the creation of all three ramparts. The scale of the gathering for Sântana and the other sites indicates political mobilisation at the regional level and hints at the principal function of the largest megafort of all.

5.3 The Cornești–Iarcuri megasite

Cornești is the largest megafort in the Banat by a factor of four. It is, indeed, the largest known Bronze Age site in Europe, with a total perimeter length from the four concentric ramparts of 33 km and an enclosed area of 1,764 ha, making it four times bigger than the Valencina de la Concepción Copper Age megasite discussed in Section 4 (Szentmiklosi et al. 2011; Heeb et al. 2017; Krause et al. 2019) (here Fig. 26). While ramparts I and II are visible in the modern landscape, with heights of up to 4 m (Fig. 27), ramparts III and IV are far less visible and may have been lower than the inner banks in the past. Research at

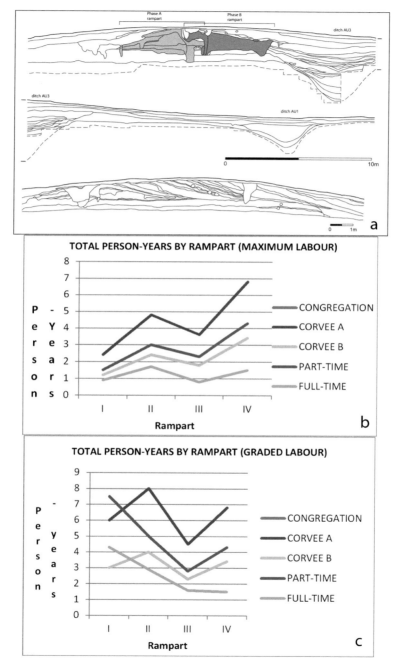

Figure 27 (a) Cross-section 2 of rampart and ditches, Enclosure I, Corneşti–Iarcuri (source: Heeb et al. 2017, fig. 2.2, re-drawn by Lauren Woodard); (b)–(c) two models of the work study, Corneşti–Iarcuri (authors)

Cornești since 2007 has relied on the three familiar techniques of investigation, supplemented by palaeo-environmental studies (OA/Nykamp et al. 2015; OA/ Sherwood et al. 2013). However, the size of the complex is daunting and the absolute dating of the sequence of rampart construction within the Late Bronze Age and Early Iron Age remains uncertain.

5.3.1 Scale

In terms of scale, there is an obvious contrast between the length and size of the four ramparts and the modest scale of dwelling features in the four enclosures. Geophysical investigations and targeted excavation both show that the highest density of features was concentrated in Enclosure II, with its antecedent features and burials placed within the second-largest rampart. More surface finds and more houses were found in Enclosure II than I, including the rare rectangular house. However, a high density of querns was found across the interior of Enclosure I, so dwelling may have been more common than previously thought. It is unclear to the excavators whether this means that there was a longer or a more intensive usage of Enclosure II or whether it was a special place for political or ritual elites (Heeb et al. 2017). What is clear is the absence of large-scale metallurgical production, although there are artifactual hints of on-site salt production. Circular cropmarks in Enclosure I may be ploughed-out barrows or house remains of the kind discovered by Molloy et al. (2020) at Idjoš. Remarkably few geophysical anomalies have been pinpointed in either Enclosure III or IV. Instead, the most complex gateway found at Cornești, with a wooden bridge across the ditch and a possible barbican, controlled access to Enclosure IV. This enclosure is partly surrounded by a defensive V-sectioned ditch but the round-bottomed ditch at another cross-section shows that defence was not always a pre-eminent function. These results show a super-abundance of open space inside all of the enclosures. While some of this space was presumably used for cultivation of einkorn, millet, emmer, spelt wheat and lentils (Krause et al. 2019), the remainder could host a regional if not a supra-regional congrega-tion of thousands of people. It is puzzling that no obvious location for a group of permanent 'Guardians of Cornești' has yet been identified, although the large house in Enclosure I currently seems the most probable place.

5.3.2 Temporality

The landscape scale is the most useful when looking at the temporality of this complex. Cornești resembles the other enclosed sites in terms of its reliance on both antecedent cultural and natural features. It is an excellent example of cumulative place-value, with limited deposition from the Early Neolithic throughout prehistory into the Late Iron Age. One ring-ditch with four ditches and a palisade dated to the Early Copper Age fell within Enclosure II, while a Middle Bronze Age occupation lay sealed under the Enclosure II rampart. Aside from the possible ploughed-out barrows in Enclosure I, a monumental barrow was located 1 km Southwest of Enclosure IV. Set within the geomorphologically stable Vînga Plain, a network of streams crossing the Cornești enclosures was active in the later Holocene through alluvial fan formation (Sherlock et al. 2013). Some gates were associated with these streams, which may have constrained movement into regular trackways, which developed into holloways through human and animal trampling.

Fieldwalking has produced evidence of Middle Bronze Age discard in the South-east part of Enclosure II, before the construction of any ramparts. The AMS dating of charcoal from the burnt remains of the Enclosure I/B rampart shows large standard deviations, with the construction of the Enclosure I rampart dated by three dates to 1411–1270 cal BC (at 95.4 per cent) (Szentmiklosi et al. 2011, fig. 3.2). The only excavated house in the interior of Enclosure I was dated to 1610–1201 cal BC (Heeb et al. 2018). Possible lanes parallel to the Enclosure II rampart suggest some degree of planning of the large rectangular houses. The thickness of the 1 m culture level inside this enclosure suggests a lengthy occupation – a notion confirmed by the discovery of Early Iron Age pottery dating to the 9th century BC in the upper stratum and confirming the coeval use of at least two enclosures. On the basis of seven charcoal dates, mostly falling in the 12th–11th centuries cal BC, Krause et al. (2019, 142 & Abb. 10) claim that Enclosure IV was built after Enclosure I. However, the contexts of these dates were not secure. On the assumption that the construction of Enclosures II and III fell between that of Enclosures I and IV, we may hypothesise the building of a new enclosure every two–three generations (fifty to seventy-five years). The explanation for the new constructions would have related to the expansion or consolidation of the Cornești regional congregation, in turn requiring the contribution of the labour of new members to striking new communal projects. There has been a deafening silence from the Cornești research teams on the question of permanent and/or seasonal occupation at the site.

5.3.3 Deposition and Monumentality

Another way of sharing the communal identity of the central place was the participation of congregation visitors in acts of deposition. However, the admittedly limited Cornești excavations have so far exposed little in the way of depositional practices. If Csanadpalota is typical of megafort deposition, a wide range of special finds in pits and ditches has been interpreted as marking ritual deposition and feasting (Szeverényi et al. 2015) of the kind to be expected at Cornești.

Conversely, the monumental aspect of the complex is shown by the vast scale of rampart construction, which has been explored by the estimation of the volume of earth required for each rampart (Krause et al. 2019) (see Table 4 & Fig. 27). Further calculation of the person-days required to excavate the earth from the ditches and pile it up on a dump rampart (Fig. 27) has examined five possible work models – the congregation model, two versions of *corvée* labour, part-time labour and full-time labour (see Online Appendix III). Although the limited evidence for permanent occupation at Cornești makes the part-time and full-time labour models improbable, given that the labour comes from the complex itself, these two models have been included for comparison with the Bil'sk study.

In the Cornești study, the labour models have been developed in two ways – a slow, gradual increase in the labour force as the enclosures develop and a starting point with the maximum labour force at the beginning – a scenario directly comparable to Bil'sk (Fig. 27). The years required for the graded workforce version increases by 50–60 per cent, with a difference of between four and eight years. But neither version required construction seasons of more than seven years for the longest rampart (Enclosure IV) and usually three to eight seasons for the other ramparts.

5.3.4 Performance and Open Space

These constructions would have formed the centrepiece of the most impressive performances at Cornești, with regular feasting and depositional events as the culmination of the completion of successive stages of the ramparts and their gateways. The variation in the density of pits in the different enclosures has yet to be explained, since excavation of these features has not yet been a priority. The paucity of geophysical anomalies in Enclosures I, III and IV reinforce the availability of huge areas of open space for congregation.

5.3.5 Congregational Catchment

The aspect of the Cornești social catchment has been the hardest variable to document, primarily because of the lack of exotica of known source(s). It certainly cannot have been coincidental that the site was located near the point where the Mureș valley exits the Carpathian ring, close to the rich metal sources of the Munții Metaliferici and the salt sources of Transylvania but even closer to local sources of copper (OA/Mareș 2002, Harta 1: added to our Fig. 24). The most complete distribution map of LBA sites in the Banat (Molloy et al. 2020, fig. 1.1) is weak on Romanian sites, yet shows a potential catchment of 190 km from Cornești to the South and South-West, with sites within 100 km to the West and North. But further research is required before we can define the Cornești congregation catchment.

5.4 Conclusions

A decade ago, Szentmiklosi et al. (2011) maintained that the population concentrated in Corneşti was insufficient to support an urban function, while there were so many gateways in the ramparts that it could not have been a defensive structure. After much new research, both conclusions remain valid: the site seems best considered as a trans-regional centre in a network of major fortified sites – a 'megasite' (Heeb et al. 2018, 395) with an emphasis on overt economic power and implicitly symbolised military power. If a military elite did indeed organise the construction of the ramparts at Corneşti, there has been little materialisation of their status, other than through the ramparts and ditches themselves. The paucity of permanent occupation features matches the criteria for its principal function as a place of congregation for large groups of people from the already large communities in sites such as Csanadpalota, Idjoš and Sântana, while this proposal is also supported by the super-abundance of open space in all four enclosures.

6 Iron Age Megasites - from Bil'sk to Bagendon

6.1 Introduction

The European Iron Age (800/700 BC–1 BC) lasted as long as the period when Trypillian communities were constructing megasites, or shorter than the total duration of the Valencina de la Concepción occupation. Yet the strongly regional series of dynamic changes in settlement and material culture underline the rapid pace of cultural change in the first millennium BC (Moore & Armada 2011). In the Online Appendix IV, we present five regional trajectories to give a flavour of the varied settlement histories that gave rise to Iron Age megasites. These trajectories share the unifying feature that the Iron Age was 'still principally a world of the common farmer' (Danielisová & Fernández-Götz 2015, 9), for whom the vast majority of settlements constituted small farmsteads comprising populations of fewer than 100 persons, each producing their own pottery, iron tools and ornaments (Haselgrove et al. 2018). These views have been generalised into the 'segmentary society' model – the default settlement unit in the European Iron Age and the polar opposite of the megasite.

The megasites that can be identified in both the Early (EIA) and the Late (LIA) Iron Age (Fig. 28; Table 5) share the main characteristics of low-density dwelling with large areas of open space within a well-defined perimeter.

The monumentality of the EIA centres was another principal characteristic (Fig. 29), embodying both the idea of construction labour as potlatch and also the rhetoric of stability and permanence despite architectural variations

The Archaeology of Europe

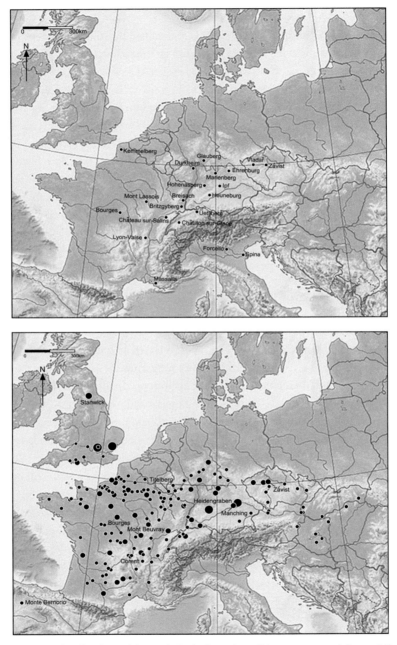

Figure 28 Distribution of (upper) Early Iron Age *Fürstensitze* and (lower) Late Iron Age oppida (source: Fernández-Götz 2018, figs. 1.1 and 2.7, re-drawn by Lauren Woodard)

Table 5 Selected Iron Age Megasites

Name & Region	Date (BC)	Max-Imum Size (ha)	Principal Features	Refer-Ence
Heuneburg, SW Germany (Fig. 29)	7th–5th centuries	100	Polyfocal centre with hillfort with unique defences, upper town and outer settlement, with monumental mortuary barrows with Mediterranean imports	Fernández-Götz 2018
Bourges, S-C. France	Late 6th–5th centuries	200	Polyfocal centre with dispersed clusters of residential areas and workshops, extending along trackways	OA/Ralston 2020
Bil'sk, Ukraine (Fig. 32)	7th–4th centuries	5,000	See Section 6.3.	
Heidengraben, S. Germany (Fig. 31)	150–80	1,660	Polyfocal complex near EIA barrow cemetery; settled area ('Elsachstadt') and huge largely empty, partially enclosed area with fertile soils	OA/Ade et al. 2013
Kelheim, S. Germany	2nd–1st centuries	600	Polyfocal complex with incomplete outer rampart, inner rampart and large area of iron mining pits with smelting furnaces and slag heaps	OA/Leicht 2000
Corent – Gondole – Gergovie, S-C. France (Fig. 31)	70–30 (Corent from 130)	3,000	Flat, fertile area with few signs of dwelling lying between three coeval *oppida* (Corent with central buildings, including Sanctuary, and 'Upper Town')	Poux 2012
Stanwick, N. England	80/70 BC–AD 65/70	270	Starts as small enclosure but expands into polyfocal centre with massive rampart in AD 1st century	OA/Haselgrove et al. 2016

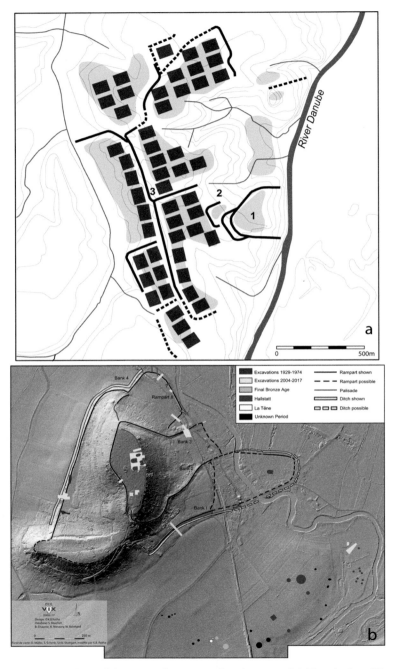

Figure 29 (a) Plan of the Heuneburg complex (source: OA/Fernández-Götz & Ralston 2017, fig. 2.1: amended by Lauren Woodard); (b) Plan of the Mont Lassois complex (source: Chaume 2020, fig. 21.1: with additions by Lauren Woodard)

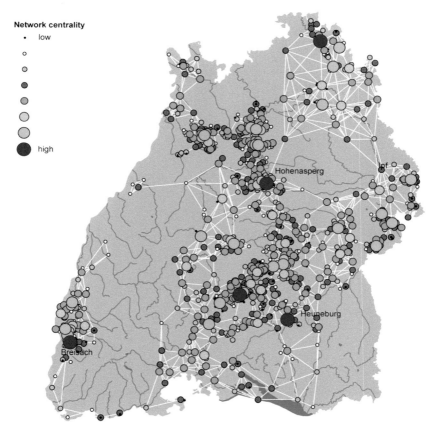

Figure 30 Map of the Heuneburg territory (source:OA/ Steffen 2012, Abb. 94, amended by Lauren Woodard)

through time. Information on Early Iron Age exchange networks, including building materials (Fig. 30), similarities in hillfort planning suggesting shared design and the diet of stock from isotopic studies all combined to suggest a congregational catchment of 60 km for the Heuneburg.

The largest LIA sites operated at a far larger scale than EIA centres, with landscape features incorporated into sites such as Heidengraben (Fig. 31) or areas of 3,000 ha between *oppida* forming coherent territories (Fig. 31). Internal *oppidum* space was highly structured, with feasting a major pre-occupation.

While the regions of the European Iron Age do not constitute unitary phenomena, the megasites are linked by their shared polyfocal development, with a marked increase in scale of occupation from the EIA to the LIA. We now turn to a classic example of a polyfocal Iron Age megasite – the largest enclosed site in Europe.

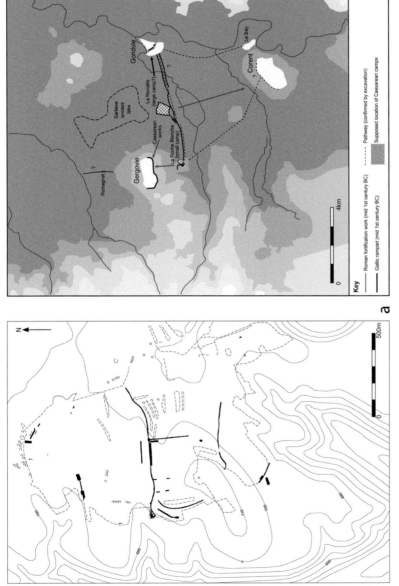

Figure 31 (a) plan of Heidengraben (source: Ade et al. 2013, Abb. 46, re-drawn by Lauren Woodard); (b) plan of the Corent – Gondole – Gergovie complex (source: Poux 2012, map, p. 259, with additions by Lauren Woodard)

Key

—— Roman fortification work (mid 1st century BC)

—— Gallic rampart (mid 1st century BC)

- - - - Pathway (confirmed by excavation)

▦ Supposed location of Caesarean camps

6.2 The Bil'sk polyfocal megasite

6.2.1 Introduction

Bil'sk is currently the largest known fortification from the 1st millennium BC in Europe (Fig. 32). It is located in the forest-steppe zone of modern Ukraine, in the watershed between the rivers Vorskla and Suhaja Grun – left-bank tributaries of the river Dnieper (Fig. 33). The site's ceramic-based chronology, including Greek

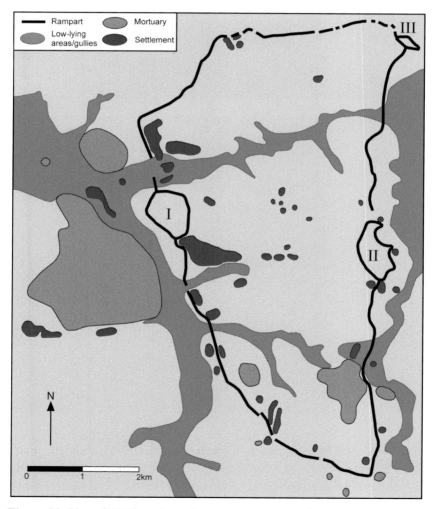

Figure 32 Plan of Bil'sk: red - settlement zones; green - barrow zones (source: John Chapman, from information in Скорий et al. (2019), Ris 299; Шапорда О. (2017), Ris. 1–2; Johnson (2020), fig. 2.3, re-drawn by Lauren Woodard)

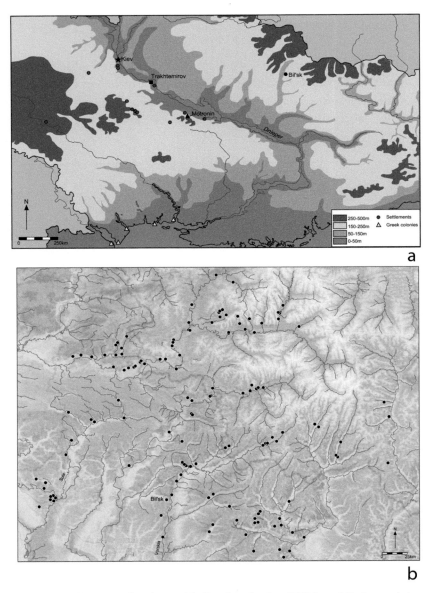

Figure 33 (a) Map of region, with Greek colonies, Bil'sk and Dnieper right-
bank hillforts (source: Johnson 2020, fig. 2.2, re-drawn by Lauren Woodard);
(b) distribution of hillforts in inner zone of Bil'sk (source: ОА/Білинський
(2018), Ris. 10, re-drawn by Lauren Woodard)

imports, show occupation in the 8th–4th centuries BC, although earlier and later interventions are also known. Palaeo- environmental studies suggest little difference in vegetation cover even at the time of most intensive occupation, although the climate was cooler and wetter (OA/Сорокіна et al. 2014). The first excavations took place in 1906 and intermittent investigations continue to this very day. The exact area of the fortification is contentious but an enclosed area of ca. 5,000 ha is unparalleled in the contemporary world. Excavation of just 0.2 per cent of the enclosed area is supplemented by remote sensing (geophysical plots (OA/Орлюк et al. 2016) and/or GIS-reconstructions (Daragan 2020)) of large parts of the site. In addition to the main rampart, there are three hillforts at Bil'sk – all structurally linked to the main wall.

6.2.2 Site Formation

Discussions of site formation have no tradition in Eastern European archaeology. Bil'sk is no exception and the complex site taphonomy is poorly understood.

The most visible parts of Bil'sk are the ramparts topped with palisades, reaching up to 9 m in height, with ditches of up to 6 m in depth (Daragan 2020, figs. 3.4–3.5 for palisade reconstructions). The other main archaeological features are *zol'niki*, barrows and *maidans*. 'Zol'niki' typified the Late Bronze Age–Early Iron Age along the Dnieper. A *zol'nik* is an ash deposit that, before ploughing, may have reached more that a metre in height (now 0.50 m), with a circular/oval shape varying between 20 and 100 m in diameter (OA/Дараган & Свойский 2018) (Fig. 34). The main archaeological contexts in *zol'niki* are cut features such as pits and semi-subterranean dwellings, above-ground dwellings and workshops. Most of the archaeological material is found within/under the fill of these cut features but also between the contexts in cultural layers. Domestic hearths, kilns, furnaces and altars are also found in the cut structures but can be free-standing (e.g. Корост 2016, 519). Traces of occupation are found between *zol'niki*, too, but have been rarely investigated. There is a contrast between the Western hillfort (WHF) with at least fifty-four *zol'niki* (OA/Шрамко 2012) and the Eastern hillfort (EHF) with none (Корост 2016: 88) but containing similar cut features without ash-deposits.

The barrows are straightforward earthen mounds, in some cases covering wooden chambers built in large pits (for reconstructions, Daragan 2020, fig. 3.6) (Fig. 34). Currently barrow size varies between 0.15–1.85 m in height, and 15–100 m in diameter (Шапорда 2017) but with loss of height. A total of 61 per cent of the 103 excavated burials contained weapons of some sort (OA/Махортых & Голле 2011), suggesting diverse identities in the buried population. *Zol'niki* have also been discovered under some mounds (Корост 2016: 359, 362, 434–6).

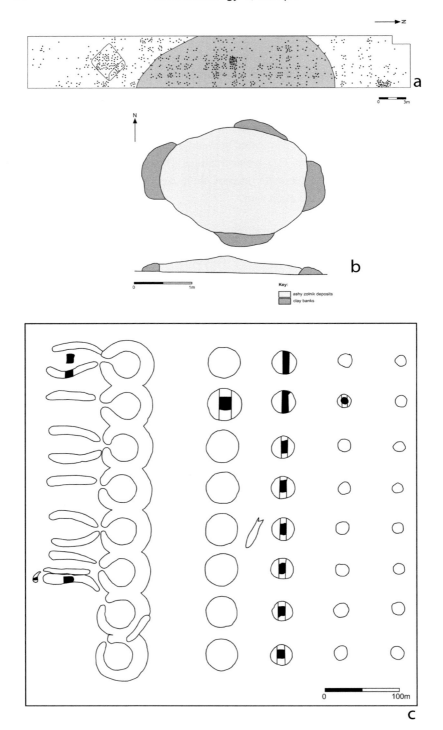

Key:
ashy zolnik deposits
clay banks

Maidans are a contentious feature class whose lack of burials suggests they were not ploughed-out barrows. They lie midway between earthworks and barrows and are best described as ring-mounds of unclear function (Корост 2016: 550). The maximum height is 4 m and diameter 330 m, with the majority varying between 0.4–1.5 m in height and 30–135 m in diameter (Шапорда 2017) (Fig. 34).

6.2.3 Site Interpretations

Within the massive 33–34 km long Main Rampart (MR), there are three smaller hillforts –the WHF (Fig. 32/I), the EHF (II) and Kuzeminskoe (III), the sequence and dating of which is hotly debated. The WHF was the earliest, built in the mid-7th–6th centuries BC in a previously settled area. The construction of both the MR and EHF are dated to the 6th century BC, with Kuzemskoe later, in the 5th or 4th c. BC (Корост 2016: 66, 132, 271). In addition, twenty-four areas were settled within the MR, with others outside, with both areas showing a still poorly understood pattern of dwelling and abandonment (Скорий et al. 2019). The wattle-and-daub above-ground and semi-subterranean houses were similar apart from the latter's central posts. Their typical settlement discard points to mixed farming practices and the specialised production of bone, metal, pottery and textiles, with such crafts organised in quarters. Significant rituals included a sanctuary for astronomical observation found in the EHF and numerous altars and pits with sacrificial deposition, some with human remains. Although over 1,000 barrows were noted ca. AD 1900, only 100 now survive, thanks to looting in antiquity and modern ploughing. Most barrows lay outside the MR, with only two groups within the enclosure. Long-term trade with the Greeks is attested by the abundant imported pottery, while links to the east and west are traced through stylistic parallels in metalwork and ceramics.

Authors disagree over the chronology (7th or 6th century BC) of the ramparts and their function – if defence, by whom against whom (for a comprehensive discussion, see ОА/Дараган 2011), and also the nature of the site. Shramko (Корост 2016: 199–201) and Bilinski (ОА/Білинський 2018) argue that local

---

Caption for Figure 34 (cont.)

Figure 34 (a) plan of zol'nik, with pit and adjacent building (source: ОА/ Шрамко & Задніков (2019), Ris 2); (b) plan and cross-section of zolnik found beneath a barrow (source: Корост, (2016), p. 436); (c) plan of barrows and majdans outside Bil'sk ramparts (source: ОА/Махортых (2013), Ris. 2) (all amended by Lauren Woodard)

agricultural communities developed a hillfort tradition, culminating in the establishment of a city-state identified by Herodotus as *Helonus* (Корост 2016: 67). Murzin and Rolle (ОА/Мурзін & Ролле 1996) see Scythians inspired by Asiatic urban centres to exert political power by mobilising the local population to build not only Bil'sk but the other hillforts in the forest-steppe. Others, like Gavrysh and Skorii, argue that Bil'sk was built by locals as a defence against the Scythians, while Liberov favours an animal corral (Скорий et al. 2019: 370–1) and Taylor et al. (2020) imply a holding point for slaves. However, none of these hypotheses can adequately explain the size of Bil'sk.

6.2.4 Scale

In an area of forest-steppe of 120,000 km^2 on the left bank of the Dnieper, there were 138 mostly small hillforts (Fig. 33), dated within the 7th–4th centuries BC, of which two (Bilsk and the much smaller Knishinvka) are dated to the 7th century BC. Although only one hillfort (Basivka) is over 100 ha, on the right bank of the Dnieper, 300 km away, there are nine more large hillforts enclosing between 100 ha and 700 ha (Fig. 33). While there were precedents for huge sites, Bil'sk's size was unprecedented. Hillfort function has been related to size, differentiated into small temporary shelters (1–3 ha), fortified settlements of relatively small tribal or territorial communities (3–10 ha: 250–500 people/ha), fortified settlements with citadels and/or suburbs (11–55 ha: 200 people/ha) and massive tribal agglomerations with short occupations (over 55 ha), some of which developed central roles in trade, handicrafts and administration and warfare, which put them on the road to local 'urbanism' (Корост 2016: 199–201).

This conflation of function, size and urbanism means that only Bil'sk is considered a 'city'. If Bil'sk was to be ranked by size of built-up area among the largest 100 modern English cities, it would come in at forty-second place – well ahead of Oxford and York – and, based on modern population densities, with a population of just under 180,000. The maximum Ukrainian calculation for Bil'sk reaches 80,000 but 50,000 is usually quoted (Корост 2016: 132). Every large hillfort is seen as a centre of its own territory, which included settlements, smaller hillforts and barrows (cf. Late Hallstatt *Fürstensitze*: see Online Appendix IV) (Fig. 36). However, Bil'sk stands out from other sites, with its 50 km^2 of enclosed area as large as the entire 'functional zone' of some small hillforts and its functional zone as large as an entire micro-regional system (Бойко 2017: 31) (Fig. 36).

We maintain that what differentiated Bil'sk from other hillforts was its political centrality, requiring large-scale seasonal congregations involving

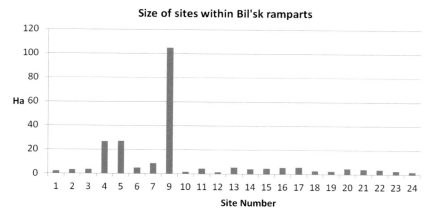

Figure 35 Size of interior sites within Main Rampart, Bil'sk (source: authors)

representatives from all its many communities, in turn necessitating a vast and impressive enclosed space.

6.2.5 Open Area

Shramko posits the maximum inhabited area at the peak of the Bil'sk occupation as 200–250 ha, or 5 per cent of the enclosed area (Корост 2016: 200). However, our calculations show that adding the areas of the two inner barrow cemeteries, the EHF (75.6 ha) and the WHF (87.7 ha) to the total area of the 24 sites in the inner areas of 239 ha produces a total area of 400–410 ha, or c. 8 per cent (Figs. 35 & 38). There were also ravines that criss-crossed the enclosure (Fig. 32) and palaeo-botanical evidence shows large areas of forests, orchards and gardens, not to mention pastureland and fields (Корост 2016: 132). Excavation bias has probably skewed the location of settlements to areas close to the ramparts but there are still zones of intensive discard well inside the enclosure. However, probing has also demonstrated the existence of open, unutilised areas (ОА/Ромашко 2017).

We argue for non-exclusive use of space at Bil'sk, not least because it is difficult to define consistently particular types of occupation across the enclosed area. The combination of all dwelling practices within the MR still left huge open areas for congregation. Part of these areas was presumably set aside for the tents of nomadic visitors. It is thus incontestable that a principal aim of building the MR was the enclosure of a huge, open, unoccupied area. This planning principle is not unknown in other hillforts, such as Trahtemirovskoe, Hodosovskoe and Zhurzhinetskoe (Дараган 2017). The only way to justify

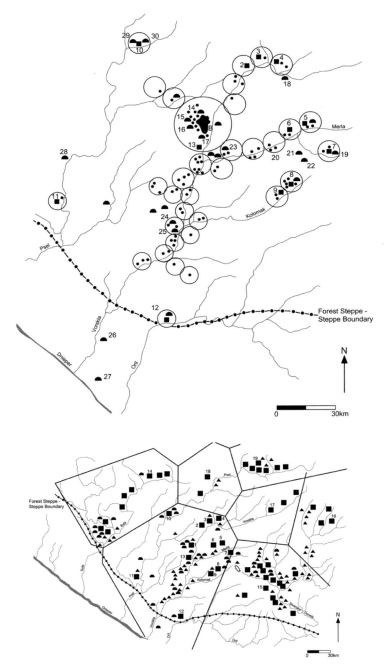

Figure 36 (upper) settlement clusters in the Bil'sk region; (lower) Map of
Thiessen polygons for Iron Age 'territories' (source: Бойко (2017), pp. 21–2:
re-drawn by Lauren Woodard)

the construction of such imposing ramparts to enclose such an area is the provision of congregation spaces.

6.2.6 Temporality

We are far from a time-slice model of fifty years' duration within an overall settlement of 300 or more years, even with closely dated imported Greek pottery. The total occupation span is estimated to last from the 8th to the 4th/3rd centuries BC, with Shramko claiming that Bil'sk was settled by locals and migrants from the right bank of the Dnieper and its maximum expansion explained by the union of tribes mentioned in Classical sources (the Geloni, Budini and Nevri) (cited in Корост 2016: 370–4). This tribal model is widely referred to in explaining the differences in settlement features, pottery and other finds between the WHF and the EHF (Корост 2016: 39, 67, 256–60; Скорий et al. 2019: 274; Бойко 2017: 18) and supports the heterogeneity of the Bil'sk populations.

Ukrainian scholars tend to treat this 300-year period in terms of continuity of dwelling, as in the example of the steady use of the EHF (Бойко 2017: 123). Such a continuous development may not necessarily have been cumulative. The duration of individual *zol'niki* (Fig. 6.7a) within the WHF varied from fifty to 150 years (ОА/Шрамко 2012), with a temporally undefined sequence of what we call 'normal' dwelling and middening, abandonment and further middening and eventual deposition of discard across wider areas (Корост 2016: 241–2). While the principal dynamic within the twenty-four inner settlements and the hillforts concerns the founding of a given settlement representing a migration from an already existing site within the main rampart (Скорий et al. 2019: 172), occasional mention is made of longer dwelling on farmsteads, abandonment of features and sequential events (Бойко 2017: 49, 54, 64; Корост 2016: 241, 519; ОА/Задніков 2019). Generally, we feel that any notion of episodic or seasonal dwelling, not to mention punctuated temporality, has been lost in the overall approach.

We maintain that differences in settlement in time and space show a combination of permanent and temporary occupation expressing the diversity of dwelling groups. Permanent occupation does not exclude temporary, repeated episodes of population influx sometimes related to congregation events.

Artifact scatters and various types of features have been identified as household units whose closest equivalent is a farmstead (cf. Western European Iron Age: see Section 6.1). The hierarchical interpretation of differences in farmstead forms and finds, with warriors on top and unfree labourers and farmers at the bottom (Бойко 2017), assumes an unchanging or synchronic view, excluding the possibility of a sequential development of such differences.

Where cyclical events are mentioned, it is in the context of historical references to the three-yearly celebration for Dionysus (Корост 2016: 372), fertility cults (Корост 2016: 394) or rituals, calendrical or astronomical observations (Корост 2016: 417) but information about participants and temporality remains vague. Seasonality is considered for animal culling (ОА/Бондаренко 2018) but the implications for dwelling are not discussed. Is it possible that the Bil'sk congregations originated in an expanded Dionysian celebration?

It is our view that the central site features – the huge ramparts – encapsulate their own dominant temporality of long-term permanence, referencing the monumentality of the barrows in contrast to the often shorter-term nature of dwelling.

6.2.7 Monumentality

The size of Bil'sk is most clearly characterised by its huge ramparts (Fig. 37). But how were they built and over what period of time? We reject Gritsyuk's (ОА/Грицюк 2004) calculations, which over-rely on a level of standardisation not recognisable in the published cross-sections, leading to the incorrect assumption of identical construction methods over the total length of the main rampart. It is difficult to relate Johnson's (2020: 208–9) work study of the Bil'sk ramparts to this study since he does not make explicit which rampart cross-section(s) he has has used in his calculations.

The aim of our work study was to make structured comparisons between the construction of three ramparts – those of the WHF, the EHF and the MR – in what appeared to be a continuous building programme that was intensified from the 6th century BC. The study is divided into two parts: a calculation of the number of person-years taken to build the three entities using four models (Table 6 & Fig. 38) and an assessment of overall construction time (Fig. 39).

It is proposed that *local full-time labour* was used to make Phase 1 of the WHF rampart in less than one year as a symbol of local identity, power and self-sufficiency (Fig. 39). Thereafter, pottery dating suggests gaps of several decades between the construction of each successive Phase, which lasted from the late 7th into the 6th century BC. For the same reasons, the same *full-time labour model* is proposed for the construction of the EHF, with the Phase 1 rampart laid out in six months and only the Phase 4 rampart taking more than one year. By contrast, the construction of the MR was a symbol of the identity and political supremacy of a much larger regional group, requiring the contribution of labour

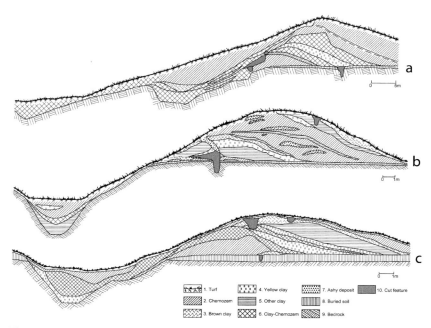

Figure 37 Cross-sections of Bil'sk ramparts: (a) West hillfort; (b) East hillfort;
(c) main rampart (source: Daragan 2020, fig. 3.4, re-drawn
by Lauren Woodard)

from most, if not all, members of the *Bil'sk congregation* over many years.
There was time for a generational gap of c. fifteen years between the constructions of each Phase of the MR, which covered the entire 6th century BC. This
modelling contradicts the possibility of rapid, massive construction in a few
years, arguing against a defensive function and in favour of community identity
and symbolic power for all three entities.

Timber for the palisades atop the ramparts of the WHF and EHF could have
been cut from the forests inside the hillforts. The same may have been true for
the forested area of 400 ha required for the MR palisade. The total earth
estimated for all Phases of the WHF combined was over 300,000 m³
(Daragan 2020) – perhaps seven times the earth required for the MR. These
daunting figures underline the monumentalisation of resources consumed as
much as labour, indicating the potlaching of labour in the context of an
increasingly impressive monument.

In contrast to the Heuneburg complex (see Online Appendix IV), there is
a remarkable divergence between the overt political statement of the majestic
ramparts and the fairly flimsy domestic architecture inside the Bil'sk complex

Table 6 Four models for the construction of the Bil'sk ramparts

Model	Work-Force	No. of Days p.a.	Local Workers	Visiting Workers	Tools and Containers	Food and Drink
Congregation	5,000	20	–	5,000	Visitors	Bil'sk + basics; visitors + feasting
Corvée (A)	1,000	50	500	500	Each supply own	Bil'sk + food/drink for all
Corvée (B)	2,000	50	1,000	1,000	Each supply own	Bil'sk + food/drink for all
Part-time	1,000	70	500	500	Each supply own	Bil'sk + food/drink for all
Full-time	1,000	140	1 000	–	Bil'sk provides all	Bil'sk provides all

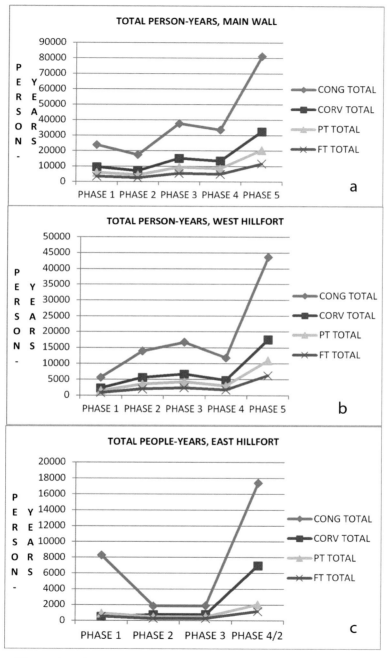

Figure 38 Three models for the construction of the Bil'sk hillforts and ramparts (source: authors)

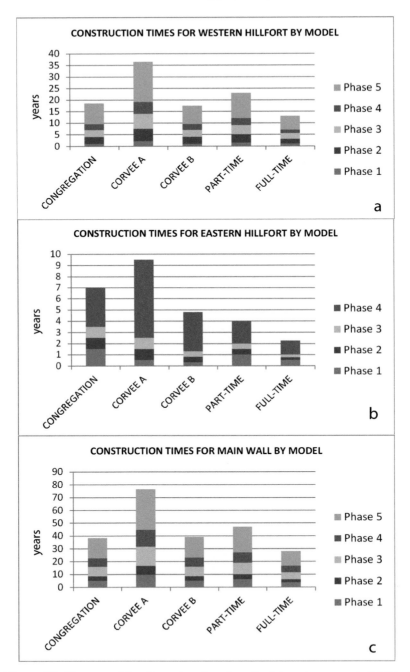

Figure 39 Three models of construction time for (a) main rampart, (b) West
hillfort and (c) East hillfort, Bil'sk (source: authors)

(Fig. 32). This contrast tells us something about the type of occupation – e.g., political elites organising a regional if not inter-regional congregation for the purposes of social reproduction, rather than a single paramount chief or a succession of charismatic leaders maintaining the might of Bil'sk for three centuries.

6.2.8 Performance

If there is one site that highlights the importance of the formalization of space allowing processions, burials, depositions, chanting, feasts with copious wine, games and competitions – perhaps involving horses – on a grand scale, it is Bil'sk. Imagine the awe felt by a visitor from small sites and hillforts at seeing Bil'sk for the first time!

Formalised performance was central to the mortuary domain, with its overwhelming number of the Bil'sk barrows. The 130 barrows to the north-west (OA/Махортых 2012) and the ninety-nine barrows, fifteen maidans and eighteen barrow-like mounds to the west (Шапорда 2017) make the hypothesis of over 1,000 monuments very plausible. The orchestrated ceremonialism of traditional burial practices is highlighted by the formal planning of thirty-two barrows arranged in four rows each of eight barrows of decreasing size and a matching row of eight maidans (Fig. 34). This layout channelled movement, affecting perception and reinforcing staged, repeated processions. With time, the steadily increasing number of barrows would have resulted in a multifocal 'stage', where public mourning, remembrance and celebrations would have been unparalleled in the contemporary world.

Performances varied between the different components of the non-mortuary domain, including the many sacrificial deposits and the sanctuaries involving calendrical and astronomical observations. The opening 'horns' of the maidans (Fig. 34) channelled participants into the central depositional area, while the scale of middening forming *zol'niki* could reach the size of a football pitch and must have involved many farmsteads. The linear feature in the middle of the WHF (OA/Дараган & Свойский, 2018) (Fig. 40) makes sense as a processional route from gate to gate, which could also have facilitated the movement of materials between *zol'niki*. Processions around the EHF, the WHF and segments of the MR would have formed important, regular calendrical events. These graded sequences of performance – from local farmstead to site-wide spectacle – created the basic structure of everyday life as well as setting the scene for significant congregational rituals.

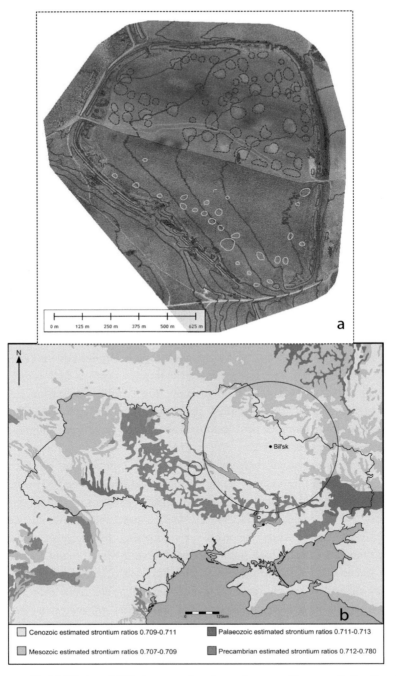

Figure 40 (a) Western hillfort processional way (source; Дараган & Свойский
(2018), Ris. 19, with additions by Lauren Woodard); (b) geological map of
surrounds of Bil'sk, with S^r pattern (source: Ventresca-Miller et al. 2019,
fig. 2.1, re-drawn by Lauren Woodard)

6.2.9 Congregation Catchment

The definition of Bil'sk's congregation catchment necessitates the navigation of socio-political narratives (discussions of class society, steppe-urbanism, historical sources, Scythian mobility) that are generally remote from our research questions. Boiko's (Бойко 2017: 21–2) division of the regional settlement system by Thiessen polygons shows Bil'sk as the centre of a 21,000km^2 area with an inner zone of 60–90 km (Fig. 36). The size of the inner zone is confirmed by Ventresca Miller et al.'s (2019) study of the strontium and carbon isotopes of Bil'sk burials, most of whom lived within 90 km of the site of their burial (Fig. 40).

The objects provide frustratingly little detail on the sources of the iron, copper alloys and gold all worked at the site but the mineralogical data suggest sources well outside the Bil'sk inner zone of 90 km. By contrast, ground stone derived from within 50 km of Bil'sk (ОА/Шрамко at al. 2018: 572).

Steady, if not constant, long-distance trade is unequivocally demonstrated by large quantities of Greek pottery, some suitable for wine and oils: 7,000 fragments and thirty-eight complete vessels were studied from 100 years of investigations up to 2014 (ОА/Задніков 2014), although Shramko mentions more than 10,000 fragments (cited in Корост 2016: 342) (cf. Greek pottery imports at the Heuneburg: see Online Appendix IV). It seems highly likely that Greek traders visited Bil'sk congregation events to negotiate the return products, whether grain, animals or slaves. However, competitors with Bil'sk included forest-steppe agriculturalists and steppe animal-breeders. The long route from Bil'sk to the Greek colonies of Berezan or Olbia meant travel over 700 km in five stages – by sea and river and on land (Fig. 33). These logistical complexities suggest that, while Greek trade was important to the provisioning of Bil'sk's elites, it was not central to its foundation.

6.3 Conclusions

Bil'sk was a colossus even by the scale of other European prehistoric megasites. Taylor et al. (2020: 622) put this in context: 'We need to simply accept that the Scythian social formation by the 5th and 4th centuries BC represented something far more militarily, and even politically, powerful than all the Greek city states put together.' For Bil'sk, this translates into a massive congregation place, whose ramparts defined open areas into which all of the other megasites discussed in Sections 2–5 would have fitted and which demonstrated the widest conceivable range of practices completed by a highly heterogeneous population. If this volume required a single exemplar of the congregational function of a megasite, we need go no further than the Ukrainian forest-steppe in the Iron Age.

7 Discussion and Conclusions

7.1 Introduction

In her recent book about capitalism, Mariana Mazzucato (2021) makes the basic distinction between profit-oriented capitalist systems and mission-oriented projects, with the US moon landing project of the 1960s the classic example of the latter. While Mazzucato identifies President J. F. Kennedy as the driving force behind the moon mission, the difference that he made to the mission once it was under way steadily decreased, insofar as its success depended on the assent of thousands of dividuals and hundreds of companies. One of the reasons that Mazzucato makes so much of the moon mission is that there have been few other shining examples of goal-oriented successes in the late 20th and early 21st century, although global heating provides a huge challenge. Can we learn anything about prehistory from the moon-landing?

In prehistory, social groups tended to be goal-oriented, viz., mission-oriented, with as many people as possible contributing to wider social goals such as the construction of a megalith or the excavation of a copper mine. In this sense, to what extent were the congregation places that we have been discussing in this Element the product of goal-oriented systems? This description fits well with three megasites defined by looking inwards from the outside – Nebelivka, with its clearly delineated plan based upon a perimeter ditch and concentric house circuits, and the two megasites defined by massive ramparts – Cornești and Bil'sk. The absence of perimeter ditches at both Alsónyék and Valencina conveys a different sense of sites defined by looking outwards from a crowded interior, in which the cumulative growth of both dwelling and mortuary features provided a forward momentum that is as close to a goal orientation as one can find there.

This answer underlines the importance of a comparative approach that takes into account the differences as well as the similarities in our sample of megasites. In this final section, we seek to draw together and compare the key elements of megasites in prehistoric Europe. We conclude by examining some basic ideas surrounding the linkages between megasites and their antecedent backgrounds as well as their internal biographies – their birth, life and death.

7.2 Why Megasites?

Why did megasites occur at all in prehistoric Europe and why were they so rare? If megasites were so vital to functioning social orders, why were there not more examples? Even with dating revisions to known monuments (e.g., the dating of the Dartmoor reaves to the Bronze Age: OA/Fleming 1988), the recognition of 'natural' features as the product of human action (e.g., the Potterne MBA complex: OA/Lawson 2000) or the expansion of LIDAR reconnaissance (e.g., the discovery of the full extent of the Greater Angkor system: OA/Evans et al. 2007), a sudden influx of hitherto overlooked megasites across Europe seems improbable. Were the megasites discussed here so different that each evolved by chance in a totally unrelated way in different millennia? Or were there common threads linking this class of site? Do they even constitute a separate 'class of site'?

Let us begin to answer these questions in reverse order. The global settle-ment research of Roland Fletcher (2019) and Kirrily White (OA/2022) dem-onstrates that 'Anomalous Great sites' (viz., megasites) occurred from the 5th millennium cal BC onwards in every inhabited continent, sharing a wide range of temporalities and practices. The long-term Holocene settlement context of seasonal nucleation at meeting sites and dispersion into the basic unit of settlement – the forager camp, segmented village or farmstead – shows the importance of seasonal aggregation as an evolutionarily stable strategy. Figure 41 shows the wide variety of megasite sizes in any one period, while underlining the gradual increase in maximum size of megasites over time. But megasites took the process of seasonal meeting several steps further into territory that had never occurred before and had to be *imagined* before it could develop (Gaydarska 2020: 36; cf. OA/Anderson 1991). This is an important parallel between megasites and the moon mission. This imagined community became far larger than any existing settlement or even any known meeting place, even though it began life as something more 'normal'. It relied on a balance of positive inter-settlement interactions over negative results, with the deposition of exotic materials and objects presencing a massive exchange network. It showed a commitment to something grand and spec-tacular while at the same time constituting a summary statement of all the important elements of the wider social network. These achievements were shared by all of the megasites in our study; we believe that, although some, if not all, aspects were found individually on other classes of site, the integration of all these developments were unique to megasites and characterises them as a separate class of site.

The rise of rare megasites would appear to be a classic opportunity to invoke the 'charismatic leader' (OA/Jones & Kautz 1981) – the prehistoric J. F. Kennedy who could integrate all of the disparate elements of the social network to form a megasite widely supported by all elements of society. However, since this explanation is unfalsifiable *sensu* Popper (OA/1959), even in the absence of spectacular single burials, we shall not consider it further. It is a lost-cause form of explanation, when all other explanations have failed.

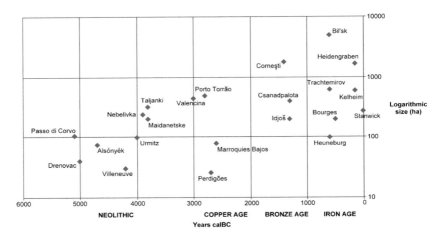

Figure 41 Sizes of selected megasites by period (source: authors, re-drawn by Lauren Woodard)

Did these imagined communities arise sporadically for different reasons in different time-place contexts? 'Yes' and 'no'. Yes, in that we would expect a set of common underlying factors causing the situation to which a megasite was an appropriate answer – perhaps concerning network issues such as access to exotics and rare skills. No, in that the response to the situation would have been shaped by different antecedent social structures and practices, not least the degree of political centralisation and the regional heritage of different classes of sites and monuments. Clearly, the change from defended tells to forts in the Carpathian Basin at the MBA–LBA transition (Gogâltan 2017) invoked very different antecedent structures and practices from the development of a mortuary congregation at Alsónyék.

However, we can observe three general aspects of the relationships between megasites and their antecedent contexts. First, there were elements of the wider landscape that were incorporated as pre-existing monuments in the nascent megasite – monuments that acted as a familiarising context for the wider region. Secondly, the 'final', grandest site form – what attracted archaeologists to the site as a megasite in the first place – was the product of the long development of a megasite's biography, which often started out much smaller and only grew into its final iteration after centuries of punctuated development and a cumulative increase in place-value (e.g., the concentric expansion of multi-ring enclosures). The positive experiences of past visitors at these places made it more likely that the advantages of scale would be further appreciated into the future. Thirdly, and perhaps most importantly, an over-riding characteristic of congregation sites is the way in which they provided a summary statement of all of the major features of the contemporary landscape – whether banks, ditches, pits, ramparts, monumental tombs and dwelling features – as well as a summary of all the key materials and objects in their regional or inter-regional exchange networks. We suggest that, in these ways, the cumulative transfer of the known into basic elements of the new and 'unfamiliar' presenced a huge cast of absent people, places and things and made the unimaginable possible. We now turn to examples of these common elements in the megasites we have discussed, beginning with antecedent features.

7.3 Antecedent Sites and Monuments

It would seem that, since all of the five megasites discussed in detail here derived from different cultural and social contexts, they would have developed out of contrasting antecedent social structures and practices. However, all of the megasites had smaller but broadly similar regional predecessors whose features contributed directly to the megasites. The clearest case was Trypillia Phase BII megasites such as Nebelivka, where a process of bricolage of plan elements found separately on earlier sites produced an integrated plan (Gaydarska 2020: 36–7). But there was an equally obvious heritage of hillforts of varying sizes prior to the construction of Cornești and Bil'sk, as well as enclosures of contrasting forms prior to Valencina and settlement sites with burial groups adjacent to house clusters in other, earlier Lengyel sites. The principal difference between the megasites and earlier manifestations was a vastly increased scale and intensity of action, which gave a profoundly different experience to visitors and residents alike. However, we can hardly claim a similar socio-political structure for all the megasites, with the antecedents of Iron Age Bil'sk already megasites in their own right and displaying signs of political centralisation far in excess of megasite antecedents in the Neolithic and Copper Age. The Late Bronze Age megaforts of the Carpathian Basin stood in an intermediate position, with a three-level site hierarchy (Molloy et al. 2020) of greater complexity than the Lengyel or Iberian sites. Yet megasites with broadly similar biographical trajectories developed out of each of these contrasting community groupings and power structures. How did this work?

7.4 Megasite Biographies (Table 7)

The main trends in the site biographies of the five megasites form a polythetic set (Table 7), with the presence of most elements at most megasites the confirmation of a distinct site class (OA/Clarke 1968: 37–8). This is not to claim homogenous social practices across all megasites: the absence of a mortuary zone in Trypillia megasites and Cornești contrasts strongly with

Table 7 Common characteristics in the growth of megasites

Megasite (Duration)	Direct &/or Local Antecedent Aites and Monuments	Biography: Changes in Size and Scale	Biography: Changes in Place-Value	Summary of Site Elements in Wider Landscape	Biography: Congregational Catchment	Summary of Exchange Networks	Goal-Orientation
Nebelivka (200–300 years)	Pollen evidence for extensive fire episode near megasite; no site, monument or discard	Perimeter ditch, inner and outer house circuits and inner radial streets in an undated sequence	Cumulative build-up towards complete plan based on inner congregation area and outer dwelling areas	All elements found (house, pit, perimeter ditch, Assembly House, Neighbour-hood, Square, Quarter)	Steady scale of 100 km catchment (spatial modelling)	All elements sparingly found (local & exotic flint, copper, gold, grindstone, manganese pigment)	Strong element of goal-orientation in overall site plan
Alsónyék (320–400 years)	Persistent place for 600 years, with mortuary focus in previous 200 years	Earliest burials in two sub-sites, with expansion of burial and settlement to all areas	Cumulative growth of fame as mortuary congregation place, reinforced by settlement	All elements except *Rondel* (house, pit, burial, ditch, neighbourhood)	Mortuary transport limit to 20 km catchment	All elements (local & exotic flint, marine shell, grindstone & axe material, jadeite, copper)	Cumulative development for mortuary congregation centre

Site							
Valencina de la Concepción (900 years)	No dated site or monument but roof stones re-used in La Pastora from earlier tomb	Expansion of burial & settlement area through the first three 200-year Phases	Multiplicity of short-term settlement & permanent mortuary sites	All elements except perimeter ditch (pit, all burial forms, dwelling discard, production area)	30 km local catchment based upon building stone	All elements (ivory – Asian and African, rock crystal, copper, flint, variscite, ostrich eggshell).	Absence of perimeter ditch limits site goals to cumulative effects of dwelling/burial.
Cornești (200–300 years)	ECA and MBA ring-ditches; MBA settlement discard and barrows	Enclosures grow from 72 ha to 17,654 ha; growth in rampart length	Cumulative increase in place-value based upon expanding congregation size	All elements except linear ditch (rampart, ditch, causeway, house, pit)	???	Poorly known (bronze)	Strong element of goal-orientation in all four ramparts
Bil'sk (300–400 years)	Settlement discard within earliest hillfort; possibly earlier barrows	Massive growth in Main Rampart, enclosing 5,000 ha, from earlier hillforts	Huge variety of mortuary and settlement sites within/outwith Main Rampart	All elements (hillfort, main rampart, barrow, *zolnik*, majdan, pit, production area)	Isotopic dietary limit of 90 km catchment	All elements (iron, bronze, gold, Greek pottery, stone for grindstones)	Strong element of goal-orientation in three hillforts and Main Ramparts

all other congregation places, while there are variable signs of local production using specialised skills (pottery at Trypillia sites, ivory and copper at Valencina, several metals at Bil'sk but no evidence for bronze metallurgy at Corneşti). Nonetheless, the centuries-long duration of all the megasites stimulated the accumulation of place-value, despite the inevitable tensions between strangers and kinsfolk and between the strategic advantages of mortuary and domestic discard, as manifested in the contrastive use of space, noted especially at Valencina.

The long duration of the megasites had another implication – the potential change in site size and use through time, as exemplified by expanding concentric enclosure plans (Perdigões and Corneşti) and the expansion or shrinkage of inner open areas on Trypillia megasites. The development of what were in effect internal antecedent features in the early megasite phases could have over-ridden other landscape features through difference (e.g., the houses of the dead at Alsónyék) or consolidated the local site heritage through emulation (e.g., the Eastern and Western hillforts at Bil'sk). These cumulative changes in morphology reinforced 'collective megasite identity' through the conjoint increase in fame of the people and their place (cf. OA/Weiner 1992), as well as the reinforcement of cultural memory enchained to megasite locales. The deposition of the largest, if undated, hoard of spearheads found at Valencina late in its sequence illustrates the impact of long-term fame and vast spatial range on the practices of future generations. The production of cultural memory was particularly striking in the emotional peaks of mortuary performances, whether the killing of cattle for ritual feasting at Alsónyék, the conjoint sensory deprivation and stimulation of entering a Valencina tholos or the participation in burial rites in a monumental barrow at Bil'sk. The cultural memory production through expanded scale of feasting was common to all megasites.

One of the most unexpected findings of this study was the discovery that megasites constituted a cultural storehouse of most, if not all, of the site and monument classes found in the wider landscape. While the temporality of this process is best understood in a preliminary way at Valencina, the cumulative recapitulation of important site classes or elements helped to sustain all megasites over the long-term by making the unknown more familiar and by strengthening the regional network linking smaller sites to the megasites. The puzzling absence of the important antecedent congregational feature at Alsónyék – the *Rondel* – although present at the nearby Zengővárkony complex can perhaps be explained by the greater emphasis on the dynamics of mortuary congregation at the former.

The other summary statement made at megasites concerned the deposition of the full range of known exotic goods and materials. This can be clearly demonstrated at Alsónyék, Valencina and Bil'sk, while the evidence is lacking at Cornești and there was a general antipathy to the deposition of exotic polished stone and metal in the worlds of clay comprising Trypillia megasites. It is surely not coincidental that the only place known so far for deposits of both Asian and African elephant ivory was also the largest congregation place known so far in the Iberian Copper Age. The 'local' catchment of the megasites for building and other heavy materials varied from 20–100 km, with the bodies of the deceased brought to mortuary congregation places such as Alsónyék or the megaliths of Valencina or Perdigões from perhaps 20–30 km. We propose that the import of more remote materials and things passed through two stages – indirect import through various sites in the 'local' catchment, which led to a strengthening of the local networks, followed by direct import by long-distance specialists to the megasite. Rather than posit a link between peaks in exotic networks and the creation of megasites, we would favour a reciprocal attraction, as in the build-up of Greek pottery at Bil'sk.

If the incorporation of summary statements of sites and monument types and exotic exchange networks was a major factor in integrating strangers and kinsfolk at the megasites, how did their personal experiences contribute to the rise, maintenance and decline of European megasites?

7.5 Scalar advantages and disadvantages of megasites: a summary

At the heart of any congregational place lay personal meetings. Megasites made possible different kinds of interactions between people, households, lineages and communities. People could meet others much more regularly, as well as meeting people they had never met before. Thus, relations of trust and friend-ship would have developed, with deeper relations through time leading not only to inter-marriage but group alliances and opportunities for political fusion. These developments would have had positive feedback effects on exchange networks, with the attraction of ever more exotic finds to specific megasites. It seems inescapable that the trial-and-error of organising hitherto unimagined congregations would have led to successes *and* failures, with failed congrega-tion sites hard to identify or distinguish from short-term settlement sites. But what makes the megasites studied here remarkable is the length of time over which they continued in use – if anything, marking generations of successful meetings. Given what could (and often did) go wrong on megasites, the long-term success of certain megasites is quite remarkable and requires recognition as the occasional triumph of sociality over increasing social entropy and the autarky and relatively short settlement occupations characteristic of much of European prehistory.

The disadvantages that megasite populations may have encountered have been summarised under the umbrella term 'scalar stress', including pollution, noise and illness, friction over decision-making and tensions over global–local identities. Moreover, the instabilities and even failures of long-distance exchange would have diminished one of the principal attractions of a megasite – the availability of a wider range of exotics than anywhere else. Indeed, the possibilities of switching allegiance to a rival congregation centre with perhaps inflated offers of potential new interactions may have damaged the prospects of a megasite with a traditional visitor base, as we suggested could have happened to contribute to the abandonment of Nebelivka in favour of Majdanetske or Taljanki. Nonetheless, we need to identify specific aspects of megasite abandonment rather than make bland assumptions about the inevitability of increased social entropy.

7.6 Conclusions

We believe that we have demonstrated sufficient commonalities between the European prehistoric megasites that we have studied to suggest that they embodied a coherent class of site, in which the best explanation of their size and scale is as particularly large examples of congregation places. Despite the long-term tensions between local relatively independent communities and congregation places, the fact that megasites demonstrated the summary statements of the full range of both sites and monuments and exotic imports showed that the populations in their catchments were well integrated into the central place – if not continuously, then often for long periods of time. It was this repeated, cumulative success in social integration that makes megasites such an important part of European prehistory. If this Element has not only improved our conversation with megasites in European prehistory but also strengthened the case for their future research funding, we can rest content.

References

Ade, D., Fernández-Götz, M., Rademacher, L., Stegmaier, G. & Willmy, A. (2013) *Der Heidengraben – ein keltisches Oppidum auf der Schwäbischen Alb*. Führer zu archäologischen Denkmälern in Baden-Württemberg 27, Stuttgart: Theiss Verlag.

Bánffy E., Oross K., Osztás A. et al. (2016). The Alsónyék story: towards the history of a persistent place. *Bericht der Römisch Germanischen Kommission*, **94**, 283–318.

Bayliss, A., Beavan, N., Hamilton, D. et al. (2016). Peopling the past: creating a site biography in the Hungarian Neolithic. *Bericht der Römisch-Germanische Kommission*, **94**, 23–91. https:10.11588/berrgk.1938.0.37150.

Bertók, G. & Gáti, Cs. (2014). *Old times – new methods*. Budapest: Archaeolingua.

Bickle, P. & Whittle, A. (eds.) (2013). *The first farmers of central Europe: diversity in LBK lifeways*. Oxford: Oxbow Books.

Chapman, J. (2020). *Forging identities in Balkan prehistory: dividuals, individuals and communities, 7000 – 3000 BC*. Leiden: Sidestone Press.

Chapman, J., Videiko, M., Hale, D. et al. (2014). The second phase of the Trypillia Megasite methodological revolution: a new research agenda. *European Journal of Archaeology*, **17**(3), 369–406.

Costa Caramé, M., Díaz-Zorita Bonilla, M., García Sanjuán, L. & Wheatley, D. (2010). The Copper Age settlement of Valencina de la Concepción (Seville, Spain): demography, metallurgy and spatial organization. *Trabajos de Prehistoria*, **67**(1), 87–118.

Danielisová, A. & Fernández-Götz, M. (eds.) (2015). *Persistent economic ways of living: production, distribution, and consumption in late prehistory and early history*. Budapest: Archeolingua.

Daragan, M. (2020). About appearance of mega-hillforts in the Ukrainian forest-steppe in the Early Scythian time: the search for an explanatory model. *Tyragetia*, s.n., **XIV** [XXIX](1), 117–39.

Depaermentier, M. L. C., Kempf, M., Bánffy, E. & Alt, K. W. (2020a). Tracing mobility patterns throughout the 6–5th millennia BC in Transdanubia and the Great Hungarian Plain with strontium and oxygen stable isotope analyses. *PLoS ONE* **15**(12): e0242745. https://doi.org/10.1371/journal.pone.0242745.

Depaermentier, M., Osztás, A., Bánffy, E. et al. (2020b). Neolithic land-use, subsistence, and mobility patterns in Transdanubia: a multiproxy isotope and environmental analysis from Alsónyék – Bátaszék and Mórágy – Tűzkődomb.

Journal of Archaeological Science: Reports, **33**, https://doi.org/10.1016/j .jasrep.2020.102529.

Fernández-Götz, M. (2018). Urbanization in Iron Age Europe: trajectories, patterns, and social dynamics. *Journal of Archaeological Research*, **26**, 117–62.

Fletcher, R. (1995). *The limits to settlement growth*. Cambridge: Cambridge University Press.

Fletcher, R. (2019). Trajectories to low-density settlements past and present: paradox and outcomes, *Frontiers in Digital Humanities*. https://doi.org/10 .3389/fdigh.2019.00014.

García Sanjuán, L. (2017). Farming economy and wealth economy in the Copper Age of the Lower Guadalquivir river: debating strategic resources at Valencina de la Concepción (Seville, Spain). In M. Bartelheim, P. Bueno Ramírez and M. Kunst (eds.), *Key resources and socio-cultural developments in the Iberian Chalcolithic*. Tübingen: University of Tübingen, 237–56.

García Sanjuán, L., Cintas-Peña, M., Díaz-Zorita Bonilla, M. et al. (2019). Burial practices and social hierarchisation in Copper Age Southern Spain: analysing tomb 10.042-10.049 of Valencina de la Concepción (Seville, Spain). In J. Müller and M. Hinz (eds.), *Megaliths, societies, landscapes: early monumentality and social differentiation in Neolithic Europe*. Kiel: University of Kiel, 1005–38.

García Sanjuán, L., Vargas Jiménez, J. M., Cáceres Puro, L. M. et al. (2018). Assembling the dead, gathering the living: radiocarbon dating and Bayesian modelling for Copper Age Valencina de la Concepción (Seville, Spain). *Journal of World Prehistory*, **31**, 179–313. https://doi.org/10.1007/s10963-018-9114-2.

Gaydarska, B. (ed.) (2020). *Early urbanism in Europe. The Trypillia megasites of the Ukrainian Forest-Steppe*. Warsaw: De Gruyter.

Gaydarska, B. & Chapman, J. (2021). Relations make the world go round: a relational approach to Trypillia megasites. In A. Diachenko, T. K. Harper, Y. Rassamakin and I. Sobkowiak-Tabaka (eds.), *Data systematization in the Neo-Eneolithic of Southeastern and Central Europe. Essays in honor of Sergej Ryzhov*. Kyiv: NASU Institute of Archaeology, 204–45.

Gogâltan, F. (2017). The Bronze Age multilayered settlements in the Carpathian Basin (ca. 2500–1600/1500 BC). An old catalogue and some chronological problems. *Journal of Ancient History and Archaeology*, **4**, 28–63.

Gogâltan, F. & Sava, V. (2010) *Sântana-Cetatea Veche. A Bronze Age earthwork on the Lower Mureş*. Arad: Complexul Muzeul Arad.

Hansen, S. and Krause, R. (eds.) (2018). *Bronzezeitliche Burgen zwischen Taunus und Karpaten*. Bonn: Habelt-Verlag.

Haselgrove, C., Rebay-Salisbury, K. & Wells, P. S. (eds.) (2018). *Oxford handbook of the European Iron Age*. Oxford: Oxford University Press. https://doi.org/10.1093/oxfordhb/9780199696826.001.0001.

Heeb, B., Lehmpful, R., Szentmiklosi, A. et al. (2018). Cornești-Iarcuri im rumänischen Banat und sein bronzezeitlicher Kontext. In S. Hansen and R. Krause (eds.), *Bronzezeitliche Burgen zwischen Taunus und Karpaten*. Bonn: Habelt-Verlag, 395–406.

Heeb, B. S., Szentmiklosi, A., Bălărie, A. et al. (2017). Cornești-Iarcuri – 10 years of research. In B. Heeb, A. Szentmiklosi, R. Krause and M. Wemhoff (eds.), *Fortifications: rise and fall of defended sites in the Late Bronze Age and Early Iron Age of South-East Europe*. Berlin: Staatliche Museen zu Berlin, 217–28.

Hurtado, V. (2006). The ditched enclosures of the Middle Guadiana basin. In A. Valera and L. Shaw Evangelista (eds.), *The idea of enclosure in recent Iberian prehistory. WAC Volume 36, Session WS29, International Series 2124*. Oxford: BAR, 109–22.

Johnson, G. (1982). Organizational structure and scalar stress. In C. Renfrew, M. J. Rowlands and B. Segraves-Whallon (eds.), *Theory and explanation in archaeology: the Southampton Conference*. London: Academic Press, 389–421.

Johnson, J. A. (2020). Trade, community and labour in the Pontic Iron Age forest-steppe region, *c.* 700–200 BC. In S. V. Pankova and StJ Simpson (eds.), *Masters of the Steppe: the impact of the Scythians and Later Nomad societies of Eurasia*. Oxford: Archaeopress Archaeology, 198–209.

Kassabaum, M. C. (2019). A method for conceptualizing and classifying feasting: interpreting communal consumption in the archaeological record. *American Antiquity*, **84**(4), 610–31.

Keeley, L. H., Fontana, M. & Quick, R. (2007). Baffles and bastions: the universal features of fortifications. *Journal of Archaeological Research*, **15**, 55–95.

Krause, R., Szentmiklosi, A., Heeb, B. et al. (2019). Cornești-Iarcuri. Die Ausgrabungen 2013 und 2014 in der befestigten Großsiedlung der späten Bronzezeit. *Eurasia Antiqua*, **22**, 133–84.

Martínez-Sevilla, F. García Sanjuán, L., Lozano Rodríguez, J. et al. (2020). A new perspective on Copper Age technology, economy and settlement: grinding tools at the Valencina mega-site. *Journal of World Prehistory*, **33**(4), 513–59.

Mazzucato, M. (2021). *Mission economy. A moonshot guide to changing capitalism*. Dublin: Allen Lane.

Molloy, B., Jovanović, D., Bruyère, C. et al. (2020). A new Bronze Age mega-fort in Southeastern Europe: recent archaeological investigations at Gradište – Idjoš and their regional significance, *Journal of Field Archaeology*, **45**(4), 293–314.

Moore, T. & Armada, X.-L. (2011). Crossing the divide: opening a dialogue on approaches to western European first millennium BC studies. In T. Moore and X.-L. Armada (eds.), *Atlantic Europe in the first millennium BC: crossing the divide*. Oxford: Oxford University Press, 3–77.

Müller, J., Rassmann, K. and Videiko, M. (eds.) (2016). *Trypillia-Megasites and European prehistory, 4100–3400 BCE*. London: Routledge.

Munro, R. (1997). Ideas of difference: stability, social spaces and the labour of division. In K. Hetherington and R. Munro (eds.), *Ideas of difference*. Oxford: Blackwell, 3–24.

Nebbia, M. (2020). Landscape studies. In B. Gaydarska (ed.), *Early urbanism in Europe. The Trypillia Megasites of the Ukrainian Forest-Steppe*. Berlin: De Gruyter, 60–110.

Nyerges, É. Á. & Biller, A. Zs. (2015). Neolithic animal husbandry in the Tolnai-Sárköz region on the basis of the archaeozoological finds from the Alsónyék-Bátaszék archaeological site, *Hungarian Archaeology E-Journal* (Winter). www.hungarianarchaeology.hu.

Osztás, A., Bánffy, E., Zalai-Gaál, I. et al. (2016a). Alsónyék-Bátaszék: introduction to a major Neolithic settlement complex in south-east Transdanubia, Hungary. *Bericht der Römisch-Germanischen Kommission*, **94**, 7–21.

Osztás, A., Zalai-Gaál, I., Bánffy, E. et al. (2016b). Coalescent community at Alsónyék: the timings and duration of Lengyel burials and settlement, *Bericht der Römisch-Germanischen Kommission*, **94**, 179–282.

Poux, M. (ed.) (2012). *Corent: voyage au coeur d'une ville gauloise*, 2nd edn. Paris: Errance.

Seager, Thomas, M. (2020). *Neolithic Spaces*, volume 2: The Bradford Archive of Aerial Photographs. Accordia Specialist Studies on Italy 19.ii. London: Accordia Research Institute, University of London.

Sherlock, S. C., Windingstad, J. D., Barker, A. W., O'Shea, J. M. & Sherwood, W. C. (2013) Evidence for Holocene aeolian activity at the close of the Middle Bronze Age in the Eastern Carpathian Basin: geoarchaeological results from the Mureş River Valley, Romania. *Geoarchaeology* **28**, 131–46.

Smith, M. L. (2008). Urban empty spaces. Contentious places for consensus-building. *Archaeological Dialogues*, **15** (2), 216–31.

Szentmiklosi, A., Heeb, B. S., Heeb, J. et al. (2011). Cornești-Iarcuri – a Bronze Age town in the Romanian Banat. *Antiquity*, **85**, 819–38.

Szeverényi, V., Priskin, A., Czukor, P. et al. (2015). Subsistence, settlement and society in the Late Bronze Age of South East Hungary: a case study of the fortified settlement at Csanadpalota-Földvár. In J. Kniesel, M. Dal Corso, W. Kirleis et al. (eds.), *The third food revolution?: setting the Bronze Age table. Common trends in economic and subsistence strategies in Bronze Age Europe*. Bonn: Habelt, 97–117.

Taylor, T., Havlicek, C. M. & Beckwith, C. I. (2020). The Scythian empire: reassessing steppe power from western and eastern perspectives. In S. Pankova and StJ. Simpson (eds.), *Masters of the steppe. The impacts of the Scythians and later nomad societies of Eurasia*. Oxford: Archaeopress, 616–26.

Valera, A. (2012). Ditches, pits and hypogea: new data and new problems in South Portugal Late Neolithic and Chalcolithic practices. In J. F. Gibaja, A. F. Carvalho and P. Chambon (eds.), *Funerary practices in the Iberian Peninsula from the Mesolithic to the Chalcolithic, International Series 2417*. Oxford: BAR, 103–12.

Valera, A. C., Silva, A. M., Cunha, C. & Evangelista, L. (2014). Funerary practices and body manipulations at Neolithic and Chalcolithic Perdigões ditched enclosures (South Portugal). In A. C. Valera (ed.), *Recent prehistoric enclosures and funerary practices in Europe, International Series 2676*. Oxford: BAR, 37–57.

Vaquer, J. (1990). *Le néolithique en Languedoc occidentale*. Paris: CNRS.

Ventresca Miller, A., Johnson, J., Makhortykh, S. et al. (2019). Mobility and diet in the Iron Age Pontic forest-steppe: a multi-isotopic study of urban populations at Bel'sk. *Archaeometry*, **61** (6), 1399–416, https://doi.org/10.1111/arcm.12493.

Videiko, M. (2013). *Kompleksnoe Izuchenie Krupnykh Poselenij Tripolskoj Kultury V – IV Tys Do N.e.* Saarbrücken: Lambert Academic Publishing.

Whittle, A. (2018). *The times of their lives. Hunting history in the archaeology of Neolithic Europe*. Oxford: Oxbow Books.

Zalai-Gaál, I., Osztás, A. & Köhler, K. (2012). Totenbrett oder Totenhütte? Zur Struktur der Gräber der Lengyel-Kultur mit Pfostenstellung in Südtransdanubien. *Acta Archaeologica Hungarica* 63, 69–116.

Бойко, Ю. (2017). *Соціальний склад населення басейну р. Ворскли за Скіфської доби*. Київ: Котельва.

Дараган, М. (2017). Городища-гиганты скифской эпохи в Украинской Лесостепи (особенности расположения и фортификации. В: *Археология и геоинформатика, вып. 8, SD-resurs*.

Корост, І. (ред.) (2016). *Більське городище в наукових працях Б. А. Шрамка.* Харків: Котельва.

Скорий С., Білозор В., Супруненко О. & Кулатова І. (2019). *Селища скіфського часу в системі Великого укріплення Більського городища.* Київ: ТОВ 'Майдан'.

Шапорда, О. (2017). Дослідження території Більського археологічного комплексу в 2016 році. *Археологічні дослідження Більського городища –* 2016. Київ: Котельва, 179–237.

Acknowledgements

Our first thanks go to Manuel Fernández-Götz and Bettina Arnold for inviting us to write an 'Element' about European prehistoric megasites and to Edgar Mendez at Cambridge University Press for seeing through the project to its completion. This Element could not possibly have looked so nice without the talents of our illustrator, Lauren Woodard, who converted our own grubby 'originals' and many other researchers' neat originals into a consistent book style. Thanks, too, to Stuart Johnston for his design of the reconstruction of the Alsónyék House of the Dead (Fig. 15). We are grateful to Knut Rassmann for allowing us to publish his geophysical plan of Drenovac (Fig. 10b). It was kind of John Watson to give us statistical advice on the Alsónyék mortuary models.

Our grateful thanks to friends and colleagues who looked at chapters about matters they know far more about than we did: Eszter Bánffy for Section 3, Leonardo Garcia Sanjuan for Section 4, Anthony Harding for Section 5 and Jim Johnson for Section 6.

Several friends and colleagues helped us with publications not so readily accessible at the time of COVID-19: Mike Seager Thomas and Ruth Whitehouse for Passo Di Corvo; Eszter Bánffy for the most recent publications of Alsónyék; Antonio Valera for research on Iberian enclosures; and Oleksandr Shelekhan and Oleksander Diachenko for Bil'sk and its settlement pattern.

Finally, we are indebted to Oleksander Diachenko for inviting us to contribute a chapter to the Sergei Ryzhov Festschrift, which he co-edited with Thomas Harper, Yuri Rassamakin and Iwona Sobkowiak-Tabaka, for it was in the course of preparing this chapter that we elaborated the relational approach to megasites. which formed the basis for the current Element.

About the Authors

Bisserka Gaydarska is a Bulgarian-born European prehistorian, currently working as a post-doctoral research assistant for the '"Project Radiocarbon" – Big Data, integrated cross-national heritage histories' at Manchester Metropolitan University. She received her first degree at Sofia University, followed by a PhD at Durham University on landscape archaeology in Bulgaria. Her broad research interests in material culture studies, landscape archaeology, inter-disciplinary studies, identity and early urbanism brought involvement in numerous field projects and research collaborations. Among them is a long-standing pursuit of fragmentation practices in archaeology, recurrent engagement with gender and personhood issues, inter-disciplinary studies that combine archeological science or information technology with archaeology (such as the radiocarbon dating of key sites in Europe), the introduction of the relational approach to early urbanism and, most recently, the Bayesian modelling of AMS dates for British prehistoric sites, including brochs.

Apart from her homeland Bulgaria, she has been involved in various field projects and museum studies in Romania, Greece, Turkey and, most recently, Ukraine, where she was the co-director of the 'Early urbanism in prehistoric Europe?: the case of the Ukrainian Trypillia megasites' Project.

Her major publications include *Landscape, material culture and society in South East Bulgaria* (Oxford: Archaeopress, 2007); *Parts and wholes: fragmentation in prehistoric context* (with John Chapman: Oxford: Oxbow Books, 2007); and *Early urbanism in Europe: the case of the Trypillia mega-sites* (author and main editor: Warsaw: De Gruyter, 2020). She has co-edited nine volumes, and (co-)authored forty-five articles and forty-two book chapters.

Since 2019, she has been Co-chair of the Archaeology and Gender in Europe (AGE) Community of the European Association of Archaeologists, editing and writing several new publications.

John Chapman is Emeritus Professor of European Prehistory at Durham University. He retired in 2018 after working at Durham since 1996, where he moved from the University of Newcastle upon Tyne after working there since 1980. He has spent his career working on archaeological theory and later Balkan prehistory, co-directing major field projects in Croatia (the Neothermal Dalmatia Project), Hungary (the Upper Tisza Project) and Ukraine (the Trypillia Megasites Project). His major contribution to theory has been the research into deliberate fragmentation of places, bodies and objects, which he has developed since 2000 with the co-author. Fragmentation research led to two books (*Fragmentation in archaeology*, 2000; *Parts and wholes*, 2007) and many articles. He has developed landscape archaeology in the Balkans, not only through the pioneering application of intensive systematic fieldwalking but also with concepts such as 'place-value', 'timemarks' and 'multi-community zones'. He has also worked intensively on mortuary archaeology in South East Europe, including one book (*Tensions at funerals*, 2000) and many articles and book chapters. He recently published a synthesis of his Balkan research (*Forging identities in the prehistory of Old Europe*, 2020).

Cambridge Elements $\equiv$

The Archaeology of Europe

Manuel Fernández-Götz

University of Edinburgh

Manuel Fernández-Götz is Abercromby Professor of Archaeology at the University of Edinburgh. His research focuses on late prehistoric and Roman Europe, the archaeology of identities, and conflict archaeology. He has directed fieldwork projects in Spain, Germany, the United Kingdom, and Croatia. Between 2015–21 he was board member of European Association of Archaeologists.

Bettina Arnold

University of Wisconsin–Milwaukee

Bettina Arnold is a Full Professor of Anthropology at the University of Wisconsin–Milwaukee and Adjunct Curator of European Archaeology at the Milwaukee Public Museum. Her research interests include the archaeology of alcohol, the archaeology of gender, mortuary archaeology, Iron Age Europe and the history of archaeology.

About the Series

Elements in the Archaeology of Europe is a collaborative publishing venture between Cambridge University Press and the European Association of Archaeologists. Composed of concise, authoritative, and peer-reviewed studies by leading scholars, each volume in this series will provide timely, accurate, and accessible information about the latest research into the archaeology of Europe from the Paleolithic era onwards, as well as on heritage preservation.

E
A European Association
A *of* Archaeologists

Cambridge Elements ☰

The Archaeology of Europe

Elements in the Series

A Comparative Study of Rock Art in Later Prehistoric Europe
Richard Bradley

Digital Innovations in European Archaeology
Kevin Garstki

Migration Myths and the End of the Bronze Age in the Eastern Mediterranean
A. Bernard Knapp

Salt: White Gold in Early Europe
Anthony Harding

Archaeology and the Genetic Revolution in European Prehistory
Kristian Kristiansen

Megasites in Prehistoric Europe: Where Strangers and Kinsfolk Met
Bisserka Gaydarska and John Chapman

A full series listing is available at: www.cambridge.org/EAE